9780716606208

Dogs, from Woofs to Wags

Dogs, from Woofs to Wags

A supplement to
Childcraft—The How and Why Library

World Book, Inc.
a Scott Fetzer company
Chicago
www.worldbook.com

Staff

Executive Committee

President
Paul A. Gazzolo

Vice President and Chief Marketing Officer
Patricia Ginnis

Vice President and Chief Financial Officer
Donald D. Keller

Vice President and Editor in Chief
Paul A. Kobasa

Director, Human Resources
Bev Ecker

Chief Technology Officer
Tim Hardy

Managing Director, International
Benjamin Hinton

Editorial

Associate Director, Supplementary Publications
Scott Thomas

Managing Editor, Supplementary Publications
Barbara A. Mayes

Manager, Research, Supplementary Publications
Cheryl Graham

Senior Editor
Kristina Vaicikonis

Manager, Editorial Operations (Rights & Permissions)
Loranne K. Shields

Manager, Indexing Services
David Pofelski

Administrative Assistant
Ethel Matthews

Graphics and Design

Associate Director
Sandra M. Dyrlund

Associate Manager, Design
Brenda B. Tropinski

Senior Designer
Don Di Sante

Associate Manager, Photography
Tom Evans

Photographs Editor
Kathy Creech

Coordinator
Matt Carrington

Production

Director, Manufacturing and Pre-Press
Carma Fazio

Manufacturing Manager
Steven K. Hueppchen

Production/Technology Manager
Anne Fritzinger

Proofreader
Emilie Schrage

Marketing

Chief Marketing Officer
Patricia Ginnis

Director, Direct Marketing
Mark R. Willy

Marketing Analyst
Zofia Kulik

For information about other World Book publications, visit our Web site at **www.worldbook.com** or call **1-800-WORLDBK (967-5325)**. For information about sales to schools and libraries, call **1-800-975-3250 (United States)**, or **1-800-837-5365 (Canada)**.

© 2008 World Book, Inc. All rights reserved. This volume may not be reproduced in whole or in part in any form without prior written permission from the publisher.

CHILDCRAFT, CHILDCRAFT—THE HOW AND WHY LIBRARY, and the GLOBE DEVICE are registered trademarks or trademarks of World Book, Inc.

Library of Congress Cataloging-in-Publication Data

World Book, Inc.
233 N. Michigan Ave.
Chicago, IL 60601

Printed in the
United States of America

1 2 3 4 5 12 11 10 09 08

Dogs, from woofs to wags : a supplement to Childcraft, the how and why library.
    p. cm.
  Summary: "Introduction to dogs, including how they came to live with people, the various breeds of dogs, how dogs help people, dogs in art and entertainment, and raising and training a dog, as told through stories, photographs, and illustrations. Features include fun facts, a glossary, a resource list, and an index"--Provided by publisher.
  Includes bibliographical references and index.
  ISBN 978-0-7166-0620-8
  1. Dogs--Juvenile literature. I. World Book, Inc. II. Childcraft.
SF426.5.D644 2008
636.7--dc22
                                     2008004434

Contents

8   What Is a Dog?
A dog is a curious nose, a seldom-still tail, and a great many other lovable things

18   Mutts and Purebreds
Everyday pooches and purebred dogs, and what makes them different from each other

54   Dogs Through the Ages
The first dogs adopted people, and people changed them from wolflike animals into the many different breeds we know today

82   Dogs to Remember
Dogs that became heroes because of their bravery or loyalty

102   Dogs in Art and Proverb
Dogs have appeared in works of art and in forms of speech throughout the centuries

112   Working Dogs and Show Dogs
Dogs are shepherds, actors, detectives, helpers for disabled people, stars in dog shows, and so much more

140   Dogs in Myth and Legend
Stories of strange and magical dogs from Australia, Greece, Japan, and other parts of the world

152   You and Your Dog
What you should know about choosing, caring for, training, and loving your dog

174   Dogs to Know
The breeds presently registered or recognized by the American Kennel Club

202   Find Out More

203   Glossary

206   Index

Acknowledgments

The publishers of *Childcraft* gratefully acknowledge the sources below for the stories and photographs in this volume. All illustrations are the exclusive property of the publishers of *Childcraft*.

Covers
Aristocrat, Discovery, International and
Standard Bindings:
    John Sandford
Heritage Binding: © iofoto/Shutterstock;
    © Clara Natoli, Shutterstock;
    © PhotoLink/Getty Images;
    © Anna Dzondzua, Shutterstock
Rainbow Binding:
    © Petra Wegner, Alamy Images;
    © Shutterstock

2-3	© Getty Images
6-7	© Shutterstock
8-9	© Jupiterimages/Alamy Images; © V/Stock Alamy Images
10-11	© Shutterstock; © Butch Martin, Getty Images
12-13	© Shutterstock; © Gary Randall, Getty Images
14-15	© Javier Pierini, Getty Images; © Shutterstock
16-17	© Shutterstock; © Lars Klove, Getty Images
18-19	© imagebroker/Alamy Images; © Shutterstock
20-21	© Shutterstock
22-23	AP/Wide World; © Shutterstock
54-55	© Creatas/SuperStock; © Photolink/Getty Images
56-65	"Four-Legs" © 1974 by Tom McGowen
70-75	© Shutterstock
76-77	©Shutterstock; © Arco Images/Alamy Images
80-81	© Shutterstock; ©Alamy Images
82-83	© Jo Sax, Getty Images; © Corbis/Bettman*
86-87	© Arch White, Alamy Images
88-89	Connecticut State Military Department
92-93	Colleen Paige Foundation
94-99	© Corbis/Bettmann
100-101	© Kim Heacox from Peter Arnold, Inc.
102-103	*The Flea-Catcher* (1655), oil on canvas by Gerard ter Borch, Alte Pinakothek, Munich, Germany (Bridgeman Art Library/Getty Images); © Digital Vision/Alamy Images
104-105	© Robert J. Preston, Alamy Images; AP/Wide World
106-107	Museum of Archeology, Florence, Italy (SCALA); National Museum of Naples, Italy (Bridgeman Art Library/Getty Images); © SuperStock
108-109	© Shutterstock; *The Children of King Charles I of England and Queen Henrietta Maria* (1637), oil on canvas by Anthony van Dyck; © Collection of the Earl of Pembroke, Wilton House, England (Bridgeman Art Library/Getty Images); *Dog Lying in the Snow* (1911), oil on canvas by Franz Marc; Stadelsches Kunstinstitut, Frankfurt, Germany (SuperStock)
110-111	© Shutterstock
112-113	© Mint Photography/Alamy Images; © Alamy Images
114-117	AP/Wide World
118-119	Assistance Dogs of America, Inc.; © Shutterstock
120-121	© Mario Tama, Reportage/Getty Images; AP/Wide World
122-123	AP/Wide World; Andrea Booher, FEMA
124-125	© Steve Smith, Getty Images; AP/Wide World
126-127	© Alamy Image; © Pictorial Press Ltd./Alamy Images
128-129	© Hulton Archive/Getty Images; © Pictorial Press Ltd./Alamy Images; © Kobal Collection
130-131	© Mike Abrahams, Alamy Images
132-133	© Mike Segar, Landov; © Mario Tama, Getty Images
134-135	© Daniel Dempster, Alamy Images
136-139	AP/Wide World
140-141	© John Sylvester, Getty Images; © Danita Delimont/Alamy Images
152-153	© Jupiter Image/Alamy Images; © Shutterstock
154-155	© Shutterstock
156-157	© Joseph H. Bailey, Getty Images; © Shutterstock
158-159	© Shutterstock
160-161	© Linda Bearden; © Mike and Laura Follenweider; © Shutterstock
162-163	© Steve Lyne, Dorling Kindersley; © Shutterstock
164-165	© Steve Short, Dorling Kindersley; © Tracy Morgan, Dorling Kindersley
168-169	© Tim Ridley, Dorling Kindersley; © Tracy Morgan, Dorling Kindersley; © David Ward, Dorling Kindersley
170-171	© Tim Ridley, Dorling Kindersley; © Tracy Morgan, Dorling Kindersley; © Shutterstock
172-173	© Tim Ridley, Dorling Kindersley; © Don Di Sante
174-175	© Shutterstock; © Barbara Peacock, Getty Images

Preface

People have trained and made pets of many kinds of animals. But the very first animal that was trained to live with and help people—the first animal to be *domesticated*—was the dog.

The one thing that makes dogs different from all other domesticated animals is that dogs adopted people, rather than the other way around. And dogs have stayed with people because they wanted to, not because they were made to. Why? No one really knows. What we do know is that the dog has been a faithful friend and loyal companion to people for thousands and thousands of years.

Here, then, is a book about these wonderful creatures we call dogs. It's about purebred dogs and mutts, about heroic dogs and famous dogs, about working dogs and show dogs. It's about dogs in myths and legends, dogs in art, and dogs in our everyday speech. It's also about choosing a dog, training it, taking care of it, and, most important of all, loving it.

What Is a Dog?

A dog is
four furry paws,
two bright eyes,
and a wet tongue ...

What Is a Dog?

... A dog is
a tail that's always moving,
an ever-curious, searching nose,
and an ear cocked up
for all the sounds of the world ...

What Is a Dog?

... A dog is
a flashing streak
of fun on the run,
and a flop-eared pooch
snoozing on a chair ...

... A dog is
one enormous appetite
that never quite gets enough,
and perfect contentment
crunching on a bone ...

14   What Is a Dog?

... A dog is
a dirt-slinging digger,
a fun-loving clown,
a sad-eyed bundle of sympathy ...

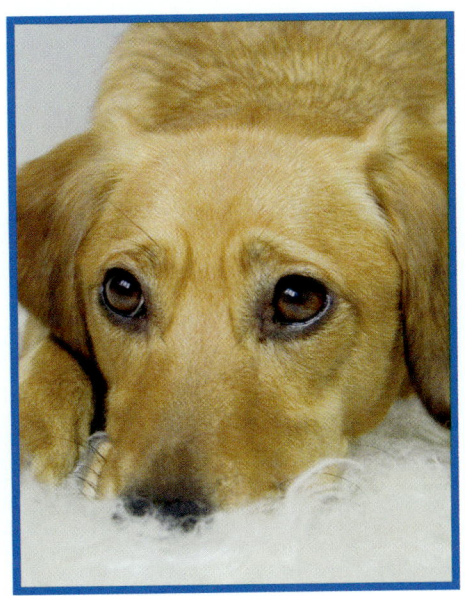

... And every dog is born to be somebody's friend!

What Is a Dog?

17

Crossbreds and purebreds

Have you ever heard of a dog called a goldendoodle? That's the name for a dog that is half golden retriever and half poodle—a dog that had a golden retriever for one parent and a poodle for the other parent.

What would such a dog look like? Well, it might have the shaggy hair of a retriever, the curly hair of a poodle, or something in between. It might grow to be a large dog like the retriever or a medium-sized dog like the poodle. The dog would be a mixture of the two dogs that were its parents. It would look a bit like both of them but not exactly like either one of them.

That's what a **crossbred** dog is—a mixture of two or more kinds of dogs. For some crossbreds, such as the goldendoodle, dog breeders choose the different breeds of the parents. Many crossbreds, however, have parents of different breeds by accident.

Golden retriever   Poodle

Mutts and Purebreds

If an Irish setter **mates** with a collie, their puppies will be half Irish setter and half collie. And if, when the puppies grow up, one of them mates with a dog that is half German shepherd and half chow chow, *their* puppies will be a mixture of Irish setter, collie, German shepherd, and chow chow.

Dogs that are all mixed up like this are called **mongrels,** which means *of mixed breed.* People often call such dogs "mutts." But mongrels are just as lovable and just as smart (sometimes smarter!) than the kinds of dogs called **purebreds.**

And what is a purebred? A purebred puppy is one whose parents are both the *same* kind of dog. When the puppy grows up, it will look almost exactly like its parents. For example, if two golden retrievers have puppies,

A goldendoodle (below) is a dog with parents from two different breeds. One parent was a golden retriever and the other parent was a poodle. The goldendoodle looks a little bit like both types of dogs.

21

their puppies will all be golden retrievers. Purebreds are simply dogs that have been bred to look the same for hundreds, or even thousands, of years.

But, every kind of purebred dog started out as a mongrel! Every kind of purebred dog was at one time a crossbred dog, either by plan or by accident. For example, the purebred dog called a Boston terrier came about when someone mated an English bulldog and an English terrier. The puppies were mixtures of bulldog and terrier. And that's often how a purebred kind of dog begins. Then, over many years, the best dogs in different **litters** are mated. In time, the dogs that are born look just the way the breeders want them to look.

Most of the dogs you will be reading about in this book are purebreds. But whether your dog is a purebred or a crossbred, remember that every kind of dog is really a mixture of two or more breeds. And every dog, of whatever kind, can be a loyal and loving friend!

By late 2007, the American Kennel Club (AKC) had **registered** 157 breeds of dogs. These breeds were divided into seven groups: Sporting Dogs, Hounds, Working Dogs,

A Saint Bernard puppy sits between its mother's paws. The puppy is a purebred—it looks just like its mother.

22   Mutts and Purebreds

Herding Dogs, Terriers, Toy Dogs, and Nonsporting Dogs. There is also a Miscellaneous Class for other breeds that may someday be added to one of the seven groups.

On the following pages, you can find out more about the breeds in each of these groups.

Whether your dog is a purebred or a mutt, it can be a loyal and loving friend.

Dog Tracks

Top Dog

Which breed of dog do you think is the most popular? According to the American Kennel Club, the Labrador retriever has been the most popular dog in the United States for the last 17 years. Here are the 10 most popular dog breeds of 2007:

1. Labrador retriever
2. Yorkshire terrier
3. German shepherd
4. Golden retriever
5. Beagle
6. Boxer
7. Dachshund
8. Poodle
9. Shih Tzu
10. Bulldog

The bulldog returned to the top 10 list in 2007 for the first time since 1935.

Mutts and Purebreds

Dogs that hunt birds

Have you ever seen a dog race off after a rabbit or a squirrel? Dogs do this because they are born with the instinct to hunt. Many of the breeds in the AKC groups are hunters.

The breeds in the Sporting Group are hunters that have been bred to find birds, send them into the air, and bring back the ones that are shot. Each breed is especially good at one or more of these jobs. The test of a good bird dog is in the field. There the dogs are judged by how well they do their job.

Pointers and **setters,** for example, are very good at finding birds. It is a thrilling sight to see a pointer moving back and forth across a field, always heading into the wind so as to catch the faintest scent of a bird.

Suddenly, a frightened rabbit dashes off. But the pointer pays no attention. Its job is to hunt birds—the dog has no time to play. On it goes, nose high, sniffing the air. Then the dog freezes in its tracks, often **"pointing"** with one front leg raised. The hunter comes up, **flushes,** or springs, the bird into the air, and fires. On command, the pointer finds the dead bird and brings it back to the hunter.

Sporting Group

American water spaniel
Brittany
Chesapeake Bay retriever
Clumber spaniel
Cocker spaniel
Curly-coated retriever
English cocker spaniel
English setter
English springer spaniel
Field spaniel
Flat-coated retriever
German shorthaired pointer
German wirehaired pointer
Golden retriever
Gordon setter
Irish setter
Irish water spaniel
Labrador retriever
Nova Scotia duck tolling retriever
Pointer
Spinone Italiano
Sussex spaniel
Vizsla
Weimaraner
Welsh springer spaniel
Wirehaired pointing griffon

For more information about these breeds, see Dogs to Know, pages 174-201, and the Index.

Spaniels, as you might guess, came from Spain originally. These dogs do not work in quite the same way as pointers and setters do. A spaniel, such as an English springer spaniel, works close to the hunter, with its nose near the ground. It does not stop and point when it smells a bird. Instead, the spaniel goes into the bushes and flushes the bird into the air so that the hunter can shoot it. On command, the spaniel then races to bring the bird back.

English springer spaniel

Mutts and Purebreds

Chesapeake Bay retriever

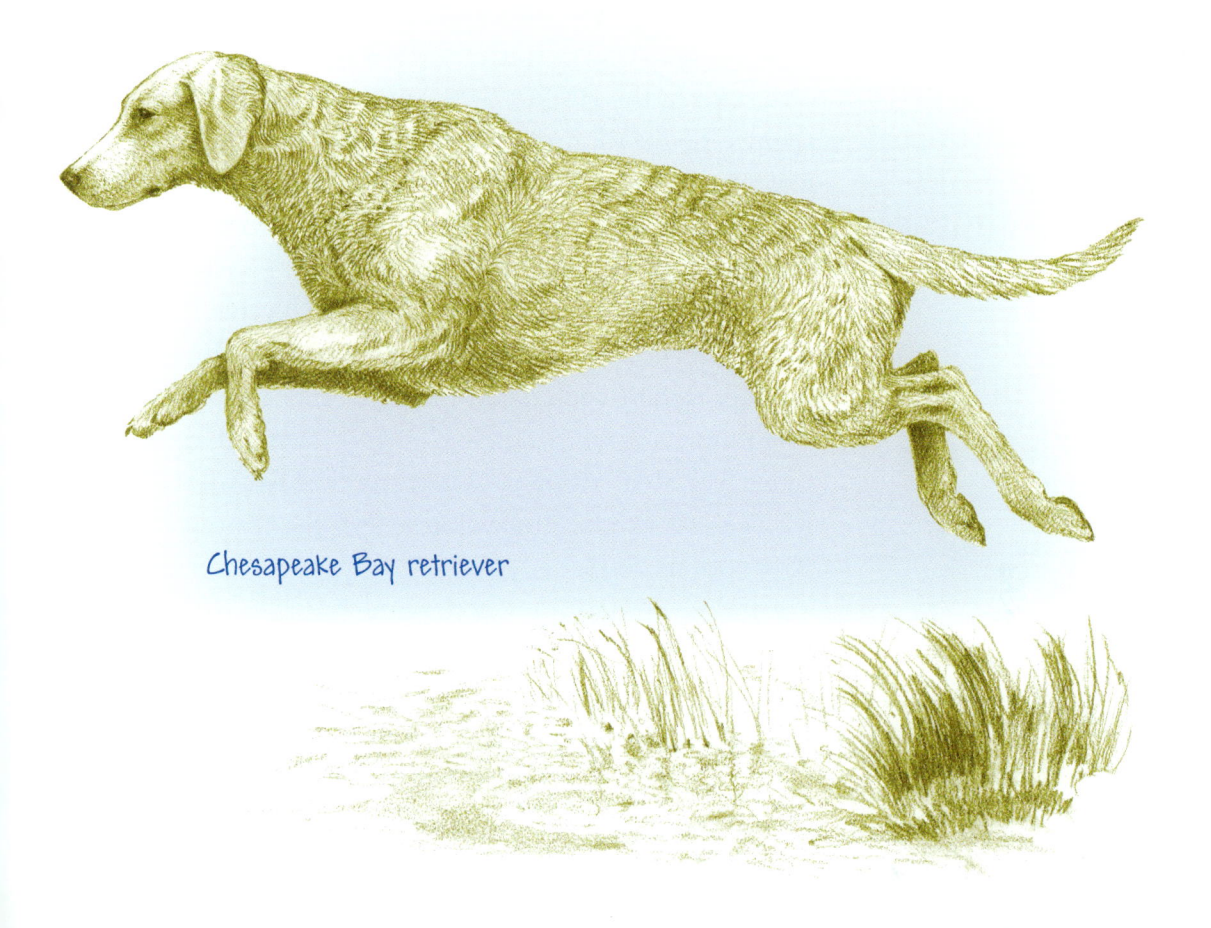

As you can guess from the name, **retrievers** have been bred to retrieve, or bring back, the birds. Retrievers are not usually expected to point or to flush. They are trained to **heel**—to stay by the hunter's side—until commanded to make the retrieve.

Retrievers work well on land, but water is their specialty. And the weather does not matter to them at all. It may be freezing cold, with a strong, gusty wind whipping up the waves. But upon hearing the command "Fetch!" the retriever will leap into the water, swim eagerly to the bird, and bring it back to the hunter. And the dog will hold the bird so gently, there won't be a tooth mark on it!

Hound Group

Afghan hound
American foxhound
Basenji
Basset hound
Beagle
Black and tan coonhound
Bloodhound
Borzoi
Dachshund
English foxhound
Greyhound
Harrier
Ibizan hound
Irish wolfhound
Norwegian elkhound
Otterhound
Petit basset griffon vendéen
Pharaoh hound
Plott
Rhodesian ridgeback
Saluki
Scottish deerhound
Whippet

For more information about these breeds, see Dogs to Know, pages 174-201, and the Index.

By sight and scent

The dogs in the Hound Group all hunt by sight or scent. The breed name often tells you what kind of animal a hound is bred to hunt.

The American foxhound, the English foxhound, and the harrier were bred to hunt foxes. These dogs work in packs and hunt by scent. As the hounds trail the fox across the countryside, they are followed by red-coated hunters on horseback. The hunt ends when the fox escapes, is killed, or hides in a hole. Many people think that fox-hunting is a cruel sport. It was banned in the United Kingdom in 2005.

Another kind of hunt is the drag hunt. In this hunt, the dogs chase after the scent of a fox instead of the live animal. First, a **dragsman** runs ahead, dragging a fox-scented sack along a trail. The hounds then follow the fresh scent until they catch up with the dragsman. When they do, they are rewarded with treats.

English foxhounds

Black and tan coonhound

Coonhounds use their keen sense of smell to hunt raccoons. They can also be trained to hunt other animals. The AKC registers only the black and tan coonhound. The American Coon Hunters Association keeps a **studbook** for other breeds, such as the redbone coon hound, the Plott, and the bluetick coonhound.

Basenji

Many hounds, such as the coonhound, basset hound, and bloodhound, have long, floppy ears. These long ears have a purpose. When a scent hound goes back and forth, nose to the ground, its long, floppy ears stir up bits of scent.

But not all hounds have long, floppy ears. The Norwegian elkhound, bred to hunt the elk, and the basenji, the barkless dog from Africa, don't look like most hounds. Both breeds have short, pointy ears and a curly tail.

Mutts and Purebreds

Hounds that hunt by sight include the fastest, tallest, and oldest breeds in the world. All are members of the greyhound family.

The greyhound, the fastest of all dogs, can reach a speed of up to 45 miles (72 kilometers) per hour. The gentle, intelligent Irish wolfhound, famous for its ability to chase down wolves, is the tallest of all dogs. It stands about 32 inches (81 centimeters) high.

The slender Saluki is thought to be the oldest purebred dog. It is also one of the swiftest dogs. This beautiful, graceful dog enjoys a special place of honor in the Arab world. Most Arabs are Muslims. In their religion, dogs are considered "unclean" (impure or evil). But the Saluki was so important to them, they declared it sacred and called it "the noble one" given to them by God.

Irish wolfhound

Bernese mountain dog

Mutts and Purebreds

Helping paws

The dogs in the Working Group were all bred to help people in their work. You might say that these dogs "lend a helping paw."

A working dog must be strong and hardy, able to do all kinds of work in all kinds of weather. The Bernese mountain dog is a good example of a working dog. This handsome, long-haired dog first gained attention as a draft dog, pulling small wagons and carts. The Bernese comes from the *canton* (state) of Bern in Switzerland. For many years, the basket weavers of Bern used these dogs to haul their wares to market.

Swiss farmers also used the Bernese to cart milk, fruit, and vegetables over steep mountain trails to busy marketplaces. At one time it was a common sight to see these big dogs at work. Even today, you may still see a Bernese hitched to a small wagon. But most are now kept as pets.

For many years, the Alaskan malamute and the Siberian husky were the hard-working dogs of the North. Teams of these dogs are sometimes

Working Group

Akita
Alaskan malamute
Anatolian shepherd dog
Bernese mountain dog
Black Russian terrier
Boxer
Bullmastiff
Doberman pinscher
German pinscher
Giant schnauzer
Great Dane
Great Pyrenees
Greater Swiss
  mountain dog
Komondor
Kuvasz
Mastiff
Neapolitan mastiff
Newfoundland
Portuguese water dog
Rottweiler
Saint Bernard
Samoyed
Siberian husky
Standard schnauzer
Tibetan mastiff

For more information about these breeds, see Dogs to Know, pages 174-201, and the Index.

still used to pull sleds loaded with supplies. Both breeds have thick, heavy coats that protect them from the bitter Arctic cold.

And what about the lovely, light-colored Samoyed? These hardy dogs once guarded reindeer for their masters in Siberia. Samoyeds still are used in sled races. Mainly, though, these big fluffy "dogs with the smiling faces" are prized by their owners as good-natured, beautiful pets.

Another mighty working dog is the big Saint Bernard. In the 1700's, this gentle giant of a dog was trained by monks in the Swiss Alps to help guide travelers through snowy mountain passes. The Saint Bernard could help rescue people lost in the mountains or trapped in snowdrifts.

Samoyed

Mutts and Purebreds

Newfoundland (Landseer, or black and white variety)

The most famous of these dogs was named Barry. You can read his story on pages 90-91.

A real hero among working dogs is the huge, powerful Newfoundland. Newfoundlands are strong swimmers and have saved countless people from drowning. In Newfoundland and Labrador, Canada, this dog's island home, the sturdy Newfoundland can still be seen pulling carts and carrying things on its back like a pack horse. But in most places, the Newfoundland is kept as a companion and children's pet. Maybe that's why James Barrie chose a Newfoundland to be the nursemaid in his play *Peter Pan*.

Collie

Herding Group

Australian cattle dog
Australian shepherd
Bearded collie
Beauceron
Belgian Malinois
Belgian sheepdog
Belgian Tervuren
Border collie
Bouvier des Flandres
Briard
Canaan dog
Cardigan Welsh corgi
Collie
German shepherd dog
Old English sheepdog
Pembroke Welsh corgi
Polish lowland
   sheepdog
Puli
Shetland sheepdog
Swedish vallhund

For more information about these breeds, see Dogs to Know, pages 174-201, and the Index.

Roundup Dogs

Do you know the famous story about a dog named Lassie? In the story, Lassie travels hundreds of miles to get back to her beloved first owner, a boy named Joe. Lassie is a collie, a breed that was first developed in Scotland, where much of *Lassie Come-Home* takes place.

Farmers used the collie to guard and herd their sheep. Collies, other shepherd dogs, and cattle dogs were bred as herders. Sometimes when a sheep runs away, the puli, a sheepdog from Hungary, jumps on the sheep's back and rides it until the sheep is tired! Then the puli herds the sheep back to the flock.

The little corgi helped English farmers move their cattle. The dogs would bite at the cattle's heels until they reached the right pasture for grazing. And, when the farmer gave the signal, the corgi could drive a neighbor's cattle away with its bite-and-chase method.

37

The German shepherd is a herding dog that might well be called a jack of all trades. This dog was first bred in Germany as a sheepdog. When there was less need for shepherd dogs, this fine animal was trained as a police dog. During World War I (1914-1918), German shepherd dogs found wounded soldiers and worked as guards and messengers on the battlefield. After the war, these dogs took on still another job—as guide dogs for the blind. And more than one has been a star in the movies and on television.

The briard, another herder, peeks out from behind its shaggy fur. These dogs come from France, where they were bred as sheepherders and guard dogs. A briard's herding instinct is so strong that sometimes it will even push against its master, as if trying to direct the person where to go!

Puli

Mutts and Purebreds

Cardigan Welsh corgi

German shepherd dog

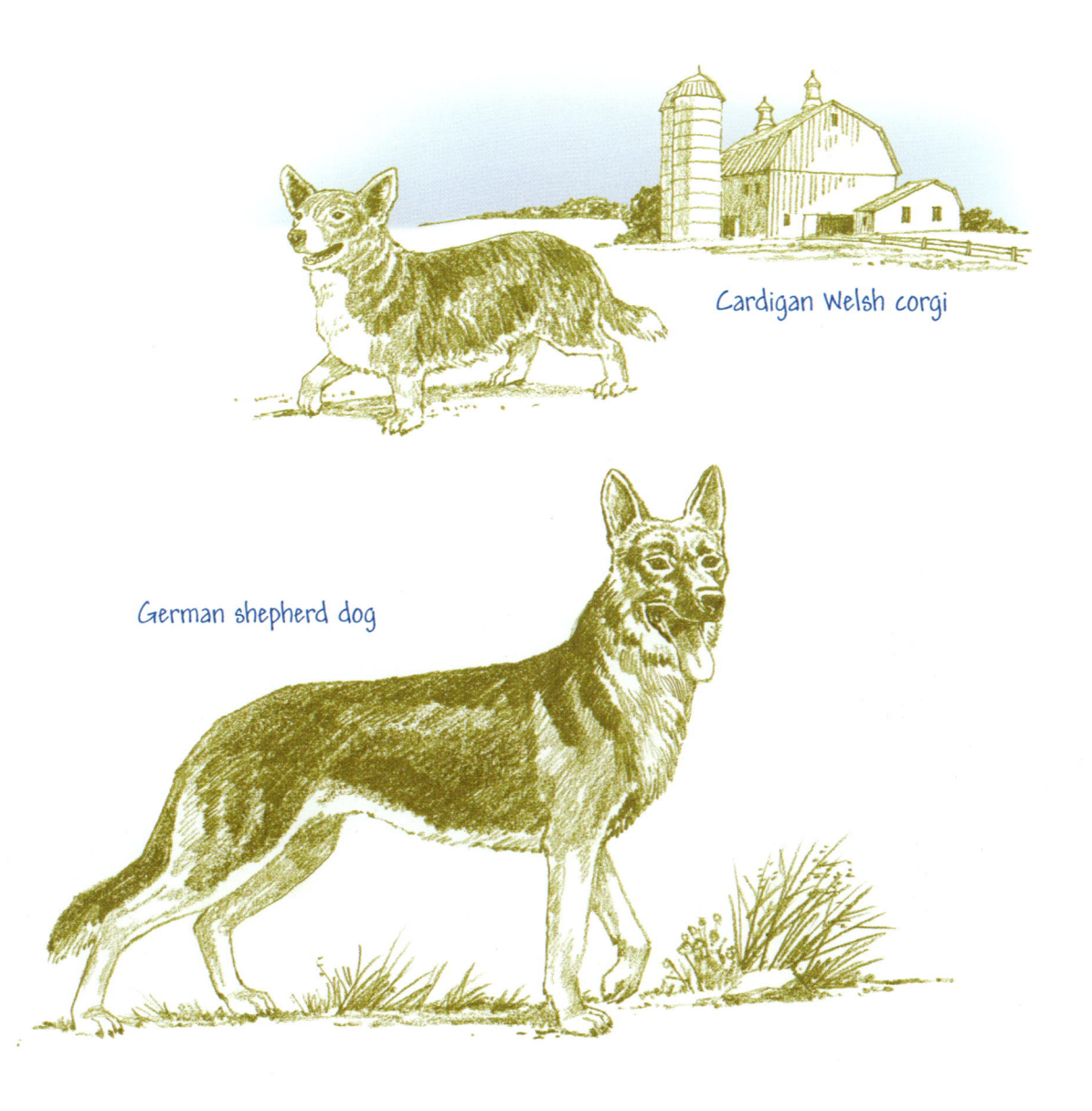

Like German shepherds, the intelligent briards have helped out in time of war. They have carried supplies to the battlefield, and they have helped soldiers find their wounded comrades.

Briards will work hard to please their masters and have even been known to "herd" young children so they don't wander off. No wonder this special dog has been called "a heart wrapped in fur."

Pug and puppy

40 Mutts and Purebreds

Small, smaller, smallest

If you have a Toy dog, or know a person who has one, then you know that these little dogs are not really "toys." Small as they are, the dogs in the Toy Group are not playthings. These dogs are called Toys because of their size.

The pug may be traced back to about 2,000 years ago. Traders brought the little dog from China to Europe about 400 years ago. It soon became a darling of the ladies at many of the courts of Europe. These affectionate little dogs with pushed-in faces are still popular today.

The smallest of all dogs is the tiny chihuahua. These dogs are named for the Mexican state where American tourists initially became aware of them some 150 years ago. Many people think the breed is Mexican, but the chihuahua was known in Europe more than 500 years ago. However, the chihuahua we know today was developed in the United States.

Long ago, Toy dogs were kept only by royalty or the very rich. The common people could not afford to keep dogs just for pets.

In ancient China, the Pekingese was a highly treasured possession of emperors and considered sacred. These dogs were seldom seen outside the palace grounds. They were often called "sleeve dogs" because their masters could carry them around in the wide sleeves of their robes.

Toy Group

Affenpinscher
Brussels griffon
Cavalier King Charles spaniel
Chihuahua
Chinese crested dog
English toy spaniel
Havanese
Italian greyhound
Japanese chin
Maltese
Manchester terrier (Toy)
Miniature pinscher
Papillon
Pekingese
Pomeranian
Poodle (Toy)
Pug
Shih Tzu
Silky terrier
Toy fox terrier
Yorkshire terrier

For more information about these breeds, see Dogs to Know, pages 174-201, and the Index.

Bulldog

Miniature poodle

Nonsporting Group

American Eskimo dog
Bichon frise
Boston terrier
Bulldog
Chinese shar-pei
Chow chow
Dalmatian
Finnish spitz
French bulldog
Keeshond
Lhasa apso
Löwchen
Poodle
Schipperke
Shiba inu
Tibetan spaniel
Tibetan terrier

For more infomation about these breeds, see Dogs to Know, pages 174-201, and the Index.

Companion dogs

Most dogs in the Nonsporting Group are now bred as pets or, as many people prefer to think of them, companion dogs. But, like most dogs, many were first bred for other reasons.

The friendly, good-natured bulldog is the national dog of the United Kingdom. It is also the **mascot** of the United States Marine Corps and of Yale University in New Haven, Connecticut. The bulldog has long been a symbol for the idea of holding on, of not giving up.

Bulldogs were first bred for the "sport" of bull-baiting. In this once-popular pastime, the dog was set after a bull that was tied to a line attached to a stake. The dog would charge in and

Chow chow

grab the bull by its tender nose; then the dog would hang on until the bull went down on its knees. This terrible and cruel practice was outlawed long ago.

Perhaps you've wondered why the bulldog's lower jaw sticks out and its nose is pushed back. The bulldog was bred this way so that it could breathe more easily while hanging on to the bull.

One of the most popular companion dogs is the bright, fun-loving poodle. These intelligent dogs are also used in many dog acts because they are wonderful performers. But the poodle was not always a pet or a performing dog. In spite of its fancy appearance, the poodle was first bred as a water retriever.

Many people think the poodle is the national dog of France. It is not, though it has long been a favorite in that country. In fact, lots of people call this dog a French

Schipperke

poodle. But the French call the poodle *caniche*. This name is short for *chien canard*, meaning *duck dog*. And in France, this dog was used to retrieve ducks.

The poodle, however, probably comes from Germany, not from France. The English name *poodle* comes from the German *pudelhund*. *Pudeln* means *to splash water* and *hund* means *dog*. So *poodle* means *splash dog*.

Poodles come in three different sizes: standard, miniature, and toy. The standard is the largest and the oldest. The other sizes were developed from the standard. Both the standard and the miniature are in the Nonsporting Group. The toy, of course, is in the Toy Group.

The chow chow, or just chow as it is usually called, comes from China, where it was used as a hunting dog. The name *chow* comes from a Chinese word that means *dog*. The chow chow is the only breed of dog with a blue-black tongue.

Today, the spotted Dalmatian is often a mascot at a firehouse. This is why: The Dalmatian is born with a love for horses, so it is not surprising that it became best known as a coach dog. These dogs once ran alongside or under horse-

Mutts and Purebreds

Dalmatian

drawn coaches and carriages. Sometimes they even ran between the horses. Their job was to chase away dogs, act as a guard, and serve as a decoration.

When firefighters began to use horse-drawn fire engines, they often had Dalmatians to keep dogs and people away from the horses and equipment. And so, though the horses are gone from the firehouse, the Dalmatian is still there. But now it is a pet and mascot.

The bichon frise *(BEE shahn free ZAY)* was a favorite of Spanish, French, and Italian royalty. Henry III, who was king of France 450 years ago, was very fond of these little dogs. He used to carry them around with him in a traylike basket suspended from his neck with ribbons. Later, the bichon was trained to entertain at fairs and circuses.

Bichon frise

Terrier Group

Airedale terrier
American Staffordshire terrier
Australian terrier
Bedlington terrier
Border terrier
Bull terrier
Cairn terrier
Dandie Dinmont terrier
Glen of Imaal terrier
Irish terrier
Kerry blue terrier
Lakeland terrier
Manchester terrier
Miniature bull terrier
Miniature schnauzer
Norfolk terrier
Norwich terrier
Parson Russell terrier
Scottish terrier
Sealyham terrier
Skye terrier
Smooth fox terrier
Soft-coated wheaten terrier
Staffordshire bull terrier
Welsh terrier
West Highland white terrier
Wire fox terrier

For more information about these breeds, see Dogs to Know, pages 174-201, and the Index.

Dandie Dinmont terrier

Digger dogs

Terra is the Latin word for *earth*, and that is where the name **"terrier"** comes from. Terriers are truly "earth dogs." These brave, scrappy dogs were bred to follow small animals into their underground burrows.

The cairn terrier is the smallest of the many terriers bred in Scotland. It takes its name from piles of stones called *cairns*. A fearless hunter, the cairn is famous for its ability to squeeze into small spaces between rocks as it goes after foxes and rodents.

Another breed of Scottish terrier got its name from Sir Walter Scott, one of Scotland's greatest writers. In one of his books, Scott told about a farmer who had six terriers, known as mustard and pepper terriers because of their coloring. The farmer called his dogs Little Pepper, Young

Cairn terrier

Pepper, Auld (old) Pepper, Little Mustard, Young Mustard, and Auld Mustard.

Many readers enjoyed Scott's story and were interested in the fearless little terriers. They even gave these dogs the name of the farmer in the story—Dandie Dinmont. And that is the name they've had ever since.

The bull terrier was bred in England as a fighting dog. Today, the "sport" of dogfighting is against the law in most countries. With its oval-shaped face and alert, upright ears, the bull terrier looks like a no-nonsense dog. The coat is either all white or colored.

Another British terrier, the Airedale terrier, is the largest of all terriers. First used to hunt small game, the plucky Airedale has proven a match for mountain lions and wolves.

Bull terrier

Airedale terrier

Australian terrier

Manchester terrier

    The Airedale has also done well in police work and as an alert guard and messenger during wars. A loyal companion and watchdog, the Airedale is very good around children.
    One of the smallest and newest of terriers comes from the other side of the world. It's the Australian terrier. Developed less than 100 years ago, these spunky little dogs have tended sheep, guarded mines, and been used by farmers to hunt snakes and rats. Surprisingly quiet for a terrier, the little Australian is a favorite house dog in many parts of the world.

Redbone coonhound

Irish red and white setter

Up-and-coming breeds

Miscellaneous Class

Dogue de Bordeaux
Irish red and white setter
Norwegian buhund
Pyrenean shepherd
Redbone coonhound

For more information about these breeds, see Dogs to Know, pages 174-201, and the Index.

There are hundreds of breeds of dogs in the world. No kennel club registers all breeds. As of late 2007, the AKC registered only 157 breeds.

Dogs of these 157 breeds can be listed in the AKC Registry, a database that includes **pedigrees** and performance records for each dog. Each year, the names of more than 1 million dogs are added to the registry. More than 45 million dogs are registered!

But what about other breeds? Will the AKC ever register any of them? The chances are that the AKC will register some. In fact, during the mid-2000's, the beauceron, the Plott, the Swedish vallhund, and the Tibetan mastiff were admitted to the AKC Registry.

To provide a step toward such admission, the AKC maintains a Miscellaneous Class for dogs of up-and-coming breeds. When there is proof of wide interest and activity in a breed, that breed may be admitted to the Miscellaneous Class. The breed may then compete in AKC obedience trials and earn obedience titles. It can also compete in the Miscellaneous Class at shows but cannot earn championship points. At the end of 2007, there were five breeds in the Miscellaneous Class.

For a breed to make it into the AKC Registry, many people must be interested in owning and working with dogs of that breed. There must be a number of breeders and at least one breed club. And all must agree on what a perfect dog of that breed looks like.

Dogue de Bordeaux

Norwegian buhund

Pyrenean shepherd

Dogs Through the Ages

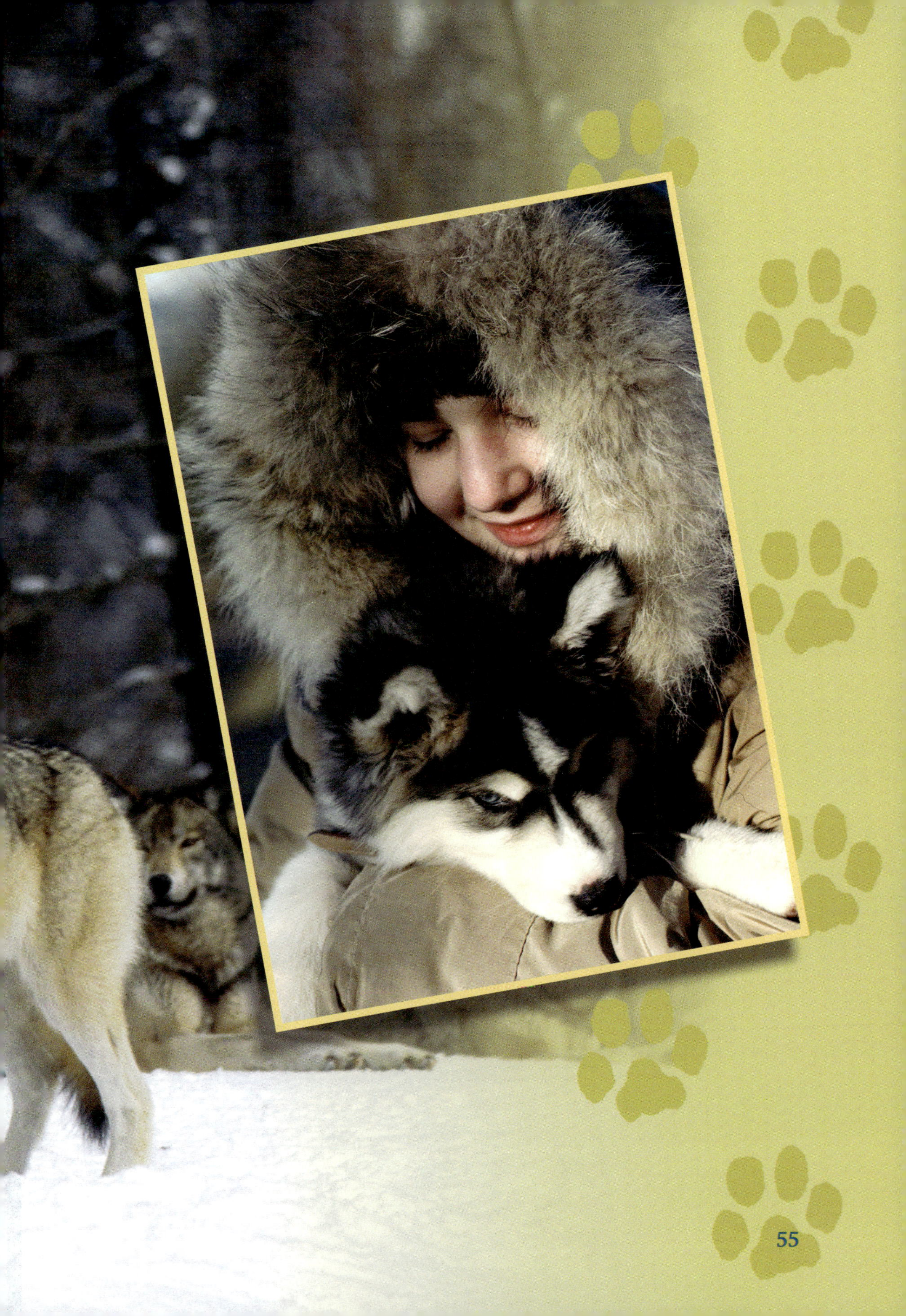

Four-Legs

by Tom McGowen

Tall-Tree had killed a fine, fat bird and was on his way back to the tribal caves when he came across the wolf cub. It was lying with the back of its body pinned among the branches of a fallen tree. There had been a storm during the night, and a howl of wind had torn the dead trunk in two and sent it crashing to the ground. The frightened cub, although unhurt, had been trapped among the branches when the tree fell.

It was a very young cub and quite small, but meat was meat. Tall-Tree lifted his spear. Then he paused. It had come to him that babies have a way of growing bigger. If he kept the cub until it grew to full size, it would provide a great deal more meat.

The thought seemed a good one, so Tall-Tree unwrapped a strip of leather that had been twined around his forearm and tied the cub's front legs together. It growled and snapped at him, but its teeth were too small to damage his tough skin. Then, Tall-Tree heaved the branches aside and yanked the cub free. It scrabbled at him furiously with its back legs until he tied them, too. Then Tall-Tree strode on his way.

Coming to the place of caves, he went to the great fire to turn over the results of his hunt as was the law. Old Bent-Leg sat before the fire, his good leg tucked beneath him. The withered one, crushed by a bison many snows ago, was stretched out. Bent-Leg kept tally on the game that young hunters brought. Tall-Tree dropped the bird on the small pile of animals near the old man's leg. Bent-Leg nodded, then jerked his head toward the wolf cub that hung from Tall-Tree's hand.

"What is that?" grunted the old hunter.

"A small four-legs night-howler," Tall-Tree replied, giving his people's name for the animal.

Dogs Through the Ages

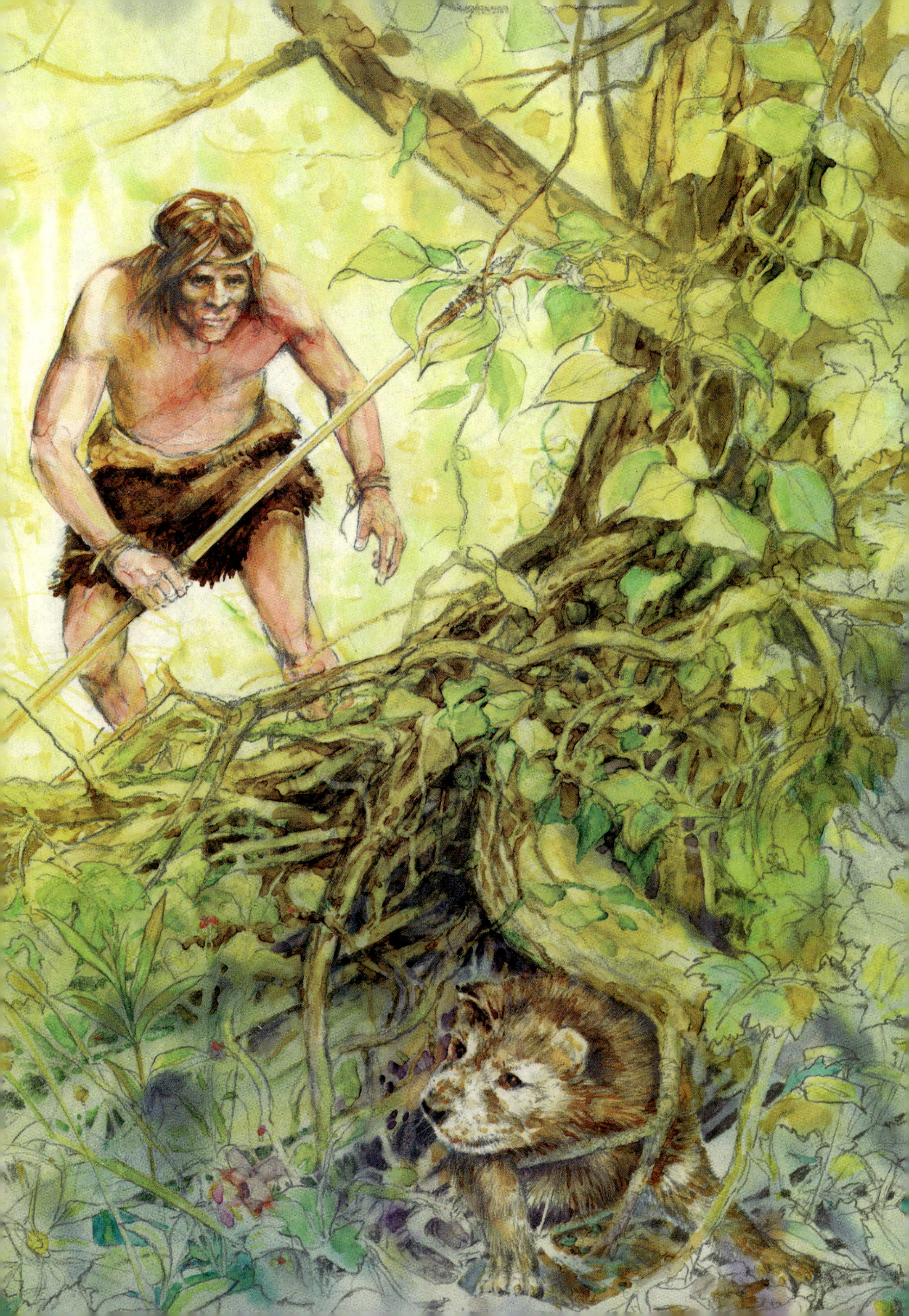

"It came to me that I could keep it tied in my cave and feed it scraps from my own food. When it is full grown, we can kill it for its meat."

Bent-Leg frowned, but realized the cleverness of Tall-Tree's thinking.

"That is good!" he exclaimed. "It is little meat now, but it will be much meat later!"

Food was always a problem for the tribe. Daily, the men hunted for animals and birds while the women and children searched for roots, berries, and insects that could be eaten. Everything that was found was shared by the tribe, and often there was hardly enough.

Tall-Tree went to his cave. Near the entrance was a large boulder, beside which he dropped the whining, squirming cub. Then from the cave he brought several thin strips of animal hide. These he knotted together to make a rope, which he quickly tied around the cub's neck, avoiding its snapping teeth. Then, with a grunt, he tipped the boulder up and kicked the free end of the rope beneath it. Letting the boulder settle back with a thump, he untied the animal's legs.

The cub rolled to its feet, shook itself, and made a dash for freedom, only to have its legs jerked out from under it as the rope pulled it to an abrupt stop. Seeing that the four-legs was firmly tethered, Tall-Tree nodded and reentered his cave.

The midafternoon sun was high and hot when he came out later. The four-legs' head was down, its tail drooped, and it panted noisily. Tall-Tree thought that if he were the four-legs, tied in the hot sun all this time, he'd be thirsty. Unslinging the animal-skin water bag that hung over his shoulder, he untied its mouth and poured a small puddle onto the ground. The cub growled faintly but inched forward and began to lap the water.

Tall-Tree frowned. He would often be gone for long trips, and he wondered how to keep the cub supplied with water during his absence. He did not want it to die of thirst.

He went into the cave for his sharp-edged digging stone. Outside again, he began chopping at the sandy soil. Growling, the four-legs backed away as far as the leather rope would let it and glared at him.

In a short time, Tall-Tree had made a hole that seemed suitably deep. He lined the hole with an animal skin, weighting down the edges with small rocks. Then he emptied his water bag into the hole. The skin held the water. The four-legs now had its own water hole, which would keep it from getting thirsty. Tall-Tree grunted in approval and left.

When he returned, he carried several meaty bones, left from his share of food at the tribal fire. He dropped these before the four-legs, although it growled at him. Later, from within his cave, he could hear its teeth scraping on the bones.

Every day Tall-Tree put fresh water into the cub's water hole, brought it scraps of meat, and cleaned up after it. As the days passed, he noticed a change. The four-legs no longer growled at him when he came near. In fact, when it saw him coming now, it would stand and watch him, moving its tail back and forth in an odd way. Tall-Tree realized the four-legs no longer feared him. He found it pleasant to have the little animal acting friendly toward him. He was surprised to find himself talking to it as though it were a child.

"Here is your meat, Four-Legs," he would call as he approached with a handful of scraps. "Are you thirsty, Four-Legs?" he would ask as he filled its water hole. The animal's ears would twitch and its tail would move back and forth at the sound of his voice.

And Tall-Tree no longer had to guard against the cub's teeth. Instead of tossing the meat and bones to the animal, he now let the cub take them from his hand. And once, as he was filling the water hole, the four-legs pushed its nose against his hand and licked it. Tall-Tree jerked his hand back in surprise. But then, hesitantly, he held it out again. Once more the pink tongue flashed out and the bushy tail fanned the air furiously. Tall-Tree grinned.

After that, he began to play a game with the wolf cub. Whenever he approached the cave, he would try to surprise the animal by coming from a different direction or by moving stealthily. But always, the four-legs would be staring straight at him, straining at the rope and beating the air with its tail.

Then, one day when Tall-Tree was bringing the catch from his hunting to the fire, Bent-Leg peered up at him.

"Is the four-legs fat enough?" asked Bent-Leg.

Tall-Tree hesitated. He had nearly forgotten his reason for keeping the cub.

"Not yet," he said, uncomfortably.

"But soon, eh?" queried Bent-Leg. Tall-Tree nodded and hurried away.

At his cave he squatted and looked anxiously at the wolf cub. It *had* grown, and before long it would be as big as it was going to get. Then he would have to turn it over to be meat for the tribe, as he had promised.

But he didn't want the four-legs to die. He knew that something had happened to him and to it. Perhaps because it had been so little when he found it, it had not grown up to be like other wolves that showed their teeth at people and then ran from them. Instead of being a wild animal, Four-Legs was more like a child that liked him. And he liked it!

The next day, Tall-Tree went hunting. He was determined to bring back more game than ever before. Perhaps, he thought, if he brought plenty of meat, Bent-Leg would forget about the wolf. But the hunt went badly. He returned with only a young squirrel. And, to his dismay, none of the other hunters had fared well, either. The pile of animals by the fire was smaller than usual.

"It is not enough!" said Bent-Leg. "We must have the four-legs now, Tall-Tree."

"Wait a few more days," said Tall-Tree. "The hunting may grow even harder. We may need the four-legs even more then."

Bent-Leg did not press him, so he hurried away. At his cave he knelt beside the wolf and rubbed its head. It nudged him with a cold nose and swept the ground with its tail.

That night, lying beside the fire in his cave, he knew that the next day, or the day after that, he would have to give the wolf to the tribe. Dreading the dawn, he fell asleep.

It seemed only seconds later that something suddenly awakened him. It was Four-Legs, snarling furiously. Tall-Tree was up and on his feet in an instant. Snatching his spear, he peered over the nearly dead fire. In the moonlight Four-Legs stood before the cave, snarling and showing its teeth, its fur bristling. Beyond it, green eyes gleamed and scales glinted on a long, sinuous body. There was an evil hiss and a rattling sound. The hair at the back of Tall-Tree's neck rose as he saw the great snake, poised to sink its poisonous fangs into the wolf's body.

Tall-Tree exploded into action. Leaping over the fire, he swung his spear forward like a club, slamming it into the snake's body, just below the swaying head. The heavy blow knocked the serpent writhing to the ground. Springing after it, Tall-Tree pounded his spear on the snake's head again and again.

After a time, Tall-Tree leaned on his spear, panting heavily. Although the snake's body still feebly twisted, he knew it was dead. Four-Legs knew it was dead, too, and stopped growling.

Tall-Tree knew what had happened. Drawn by the heat of the fire, the deadly snake had crawled toward the cave. If it had been attracted by the warmth of Tall-Tree's body, it probably would have coiled itself next to him. Had he jostled it, the creature would certainly have bitten him. He recalled when just such a snake had bitten a man. The man had raved with pain and then died. Tall-Tree shivered. If Four-Legs had not growled and wakened him, he also might have died.

Tall-Tree fed the fire until it blazed up again. Then he dragged the snake into the cave and began to skin it. When he had finished, he gazed thoughtfully at the thick coils of white meat.

At dawn, he hurried to the tribal fire, carrying the snake meat. Bent-Leg was already there, as were several hunters waiting for a lighter sky before starting on their way. Among them was Green-Leaf, the tribe's leader. Tall-Tree dumped the coils of meat near Bent-Leg's feet.

"I have meat for the tribe," he said, looking at Green-Leaf. "I will hunt for other meat this day, but I bring this meat now."

The men stared at the white coils. "Where did you find this long-crawler?" asked Green-Leaf.

"It came to my cave, seeking the warmth of the fire as long-crawlers do after sundown," Tall-Tree replied. "I killed it."

"Were you bitten?" asked Green-Leaf, looking at him anxiously.

Tall-Tree shook his head. "I might have been bitten," he said. "But the four-legs tied at my cave woke me with the noise of its anger. It saved my life." He looked into Green-Leaf's eyes. "I was going to give the four-legs as meat for the tribe. Let me give this meat instead, Green-Leaf. Let the four-legs live!"

Green-Leaf considered his words. "I do not know what an animal is good for, except to eat. What will you do with the four-legs?"

"I will set it free," answered Tall-Tree.

The chieftain thought. "It is well," he said at last. "You promised the tribe meat, and you brought meat as you promised. The four-legs saved you to hunt for the tribe. Let it go then, if that is your wish."

Tall-Tree walked slowly back to his cave. He was glad that the wolf would not have to die. Yet he felt as though a big stone sat heavily inside his chest. He knew that the moment he untied the animal's rope, the wolf would run off into the forest. Tall-Tree did not like this thought, but he felt he must set Four-Legs free. It was the only way he could repay the animal for saving his life.

At the cave, he knelt, loosened the knot in the leather rope, and pulled it off Four-Legs's neck. The wolf shook itself and looked at him strangely. Tall-Tree turned and went into the cave. He felt a wetness in his eyes, something he had not felt since he was a boy. He squatted by the fire and gathered his weapons for the day's hunt.

Something pattered over the cave floor behind him. Tall-Tree turned. Four-Legs stood just inside the cave opening. Its tail drooped and it held its head low. It stared at Tall-Tree intently.

Then the animal moved into the cave. It was a strange movement. Its stomach was flat on the ground, but the back part of its body was pointed upward. It inched forward with little pulls of its front paws. Slowly, it crept toward Tall-Tree until its nose was only inches from the man's face.

Then it licked Tall-Tree's nose.

Tall-Tree yelled with delight. Four-Legs didn't want to leave; it had said so as plainly as if it could talk! Tall-Tree rubbed the animal's head with both hands. Four-Legs flopped onto its back, and Tall-Tree rubbed its stomach. The wolf's tongue lolled out of its mouth, and its lips were pulled back into what seemed to be a grin as wide as the one on Tall-Tree's face.

After a while Tall-Tree jumped to his feet.

"Come, Four-Legs," he said. "Let's go hunting!"

Four-Legs rolled to its feet and shook itself.

Then the world's first pet and its two-legged friend happily hurried off together.

About the author:
Tom McGowen, a former Senior Editor of *Childcraft,* is the author of more than 50 children's books.

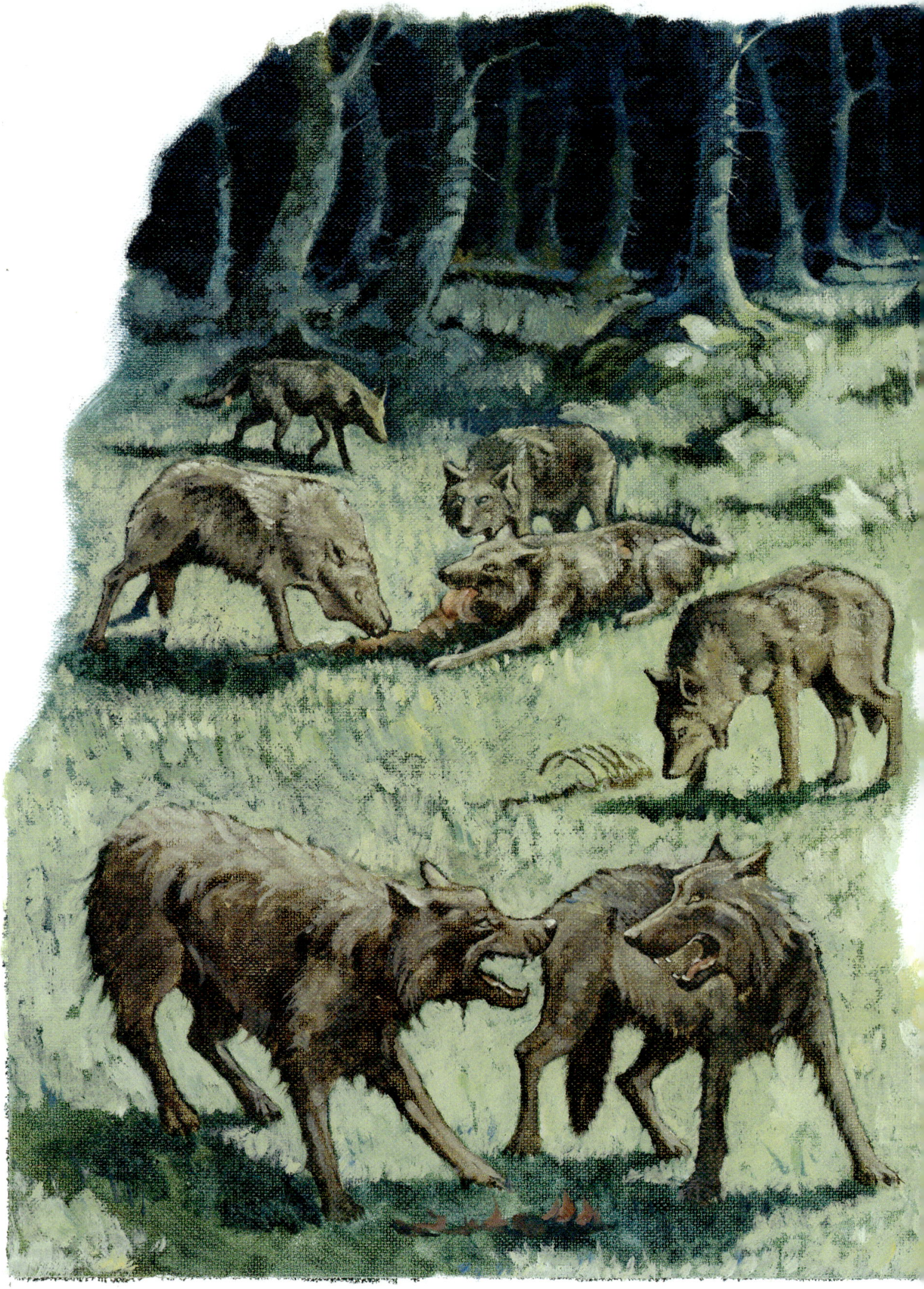

The first dogs

The gray wolf is the direct ancestor of the dog, and the first "dogs" were really wolves. How did these big, wild animals and people get to be such good friends?

Did people capture some of the wolves, tame them, and turn them into pets and helpers? No one really knows. Some scientists think that wolves and people just got used to each other over many thousands of years. Here is how they think it might have happened.

By about 15,000 years ago, there were small groups of people living in most parts of the world. These people did not live in towns or cities. They lived out in the open, in little huts, or in tents, or sometimes in caves. They hunted animals for most of their food and used nearly every part of each animal they killed. They ate the meat, made the skins into clothing, and used the bones for spearpoints, drills, and needles.

But there was always something left—bones and inside parts that people did not care to eat or could not use. And, of course, these people of long ago had no trash cans or garbage disposals. So they simply left on the ground what they did not eat or use.

Other creatures were always glad to get these leftovers. At night, while people slept, packs and families of wolves prowled about in search of food. They smelled the remains thrown away by people and crept in quietly to munch on all these good things.

There were always such leftovers near any camping place. And so packs of wolves got used to staying near the camps in order to enjoy free meals. At first, perhaps, people may not have liked having wild animals so near. They probably tried to drive the wolves away and may have even killed some of them. But the wolves simply hid and stayed close to be near the food.

In time, people probably discovered that the wolves were useful in a number of ways. If a dangerous animal, such as a bear or a cave lion, came near, the wolves would set up a great racket of snarls that alerted people to the danger. Sometimes, the wolves may have chased a deer or other animal toward the camp. Then the men would be able to kill it easily. Gradually, people learned to put up with the wolves and stopped trying to drive them away.

Dog Tracks

Small Dogs

It's not hard to understand how big dogs developed from wolves. But how did we get such tiny dogs as the chihuahua and the pug?

Scientists have discovered that all small dogs have a *mutation* (change) in the exact same *gene* (the part of a cell that determines what characteristics a living thing inherits from its parents). The scientists think that when wolves first began to approach people, the few who had this mutation were probably less threatening to people because they were smaller. So people tolerated their presence, they got more food, and they produced more small wolves like themselves. When people began breeding dogs, they deliberately mated the smallest wolves—which all carried this "smallness" gene.

As hundreds of years passed, generations of wolves and people grew up living near one another. They grew more and more used to each other. Wolf puppies that strayed close to a camp were probably picked up, played with, and fed special scraps by the children.

It is likely that many of the wolf pups stayed with the children and grew up as their pets. When the men went hunting, these grown-up wolves went along with them—and were a big help in finding, chasing, and catching animals.

That is one possible way that some wolves slowly changed and became dogs—the friendly, loyal, tail-wagging creatures we love so much.

From a wolf to a lap dog

Some kinds of dogs still look somewhat like the gray wolves that were their ancestors. The German shepherd dog looks much like a gray wolf. So do the Alaskan malamute, the Siberian husky, and the Norwegian elkhound. But a chubby, snub-nosed little Pekingese certainly does not look anything like a wolf. Neither does a long-bodied, short-legged dachshund. Why don't all dogs still look like gray wolves? Why are some dogs so different?

Most dogs do not look like wolves because dogs have slowly changed during many thousands of years. Here's how it probably happened.

Gray wolves don't all look alike. Just as there are a great many differences among people, there are many differences among these wolves. Some of them may be smarter than others, some may be stronger, and some, faster. Gray wolves also differ in their markings, the length of their **muzzle,** and so on.

If a light-coated wolf mates with a wolf that has a darker coat, some of their puppies will have light hair and some will have dark hair. But if two light-coated wolves mate, most of their puppies will have light hair.

At first these mating patterns happened by accident. Then, prehistoric people must have noticed the changes happening. So they began to mate certain wolves with traits they liked to get the kind of wolf they wanted. If only the very biggest and strongest wolves were mated, for example, most of the puppies were more likely to grow up to be big and strong, too. By doing this over and over again, people would soon have a whole group of wolves that were bigger and stronger than others. And of course, by mating smaller wolves, or by mating only light-coated wolves, and so on, they slowly got wolves that looked different from the two they started with.

    This is probably how different kinds, or breeds, of dogs began. And this helps to explain why lap dogs such as the Pekingese, hunting dogs such as the dachshund, and many other breeds don't look a bit like their wolf ancestors. These dogs were changed, little by little, during many years, until people had just the kind of dog they wanted.

Scientists have proved through the study of genes that all of the dogs we know today are descendants of the gray wolf (above), even though some dogs no longer look anything like a gray wolf.

Old breeds of dogs

People have been breeding different kinds of dogs for thousands of years. Each kind of dog was bred to do a certain kind of thing, whether it was to hunt or just to look cute. But for a long, long time, our prehistoric ancestors, whether they lived in Europe, Africa, or Asia, lived by hunting. So most of the first dogs everywhere were probably bred to be hunters.

The large, sturdy gray wolves that became the ancestors of all dogs hunted big animals. And they had heavy coats that kept them warm in the cold climate. The first dogs that came from these wolves looked much like them.

Norwegian elkhound

Scientists in Norway discovered a cave containing the bones and tools of people who lived about 7,000 years ago. They also found the skeletons of several dogs. These dogs had been big, strong animals. They probably helped people hunt such creatures as deer, elk, and even bears, for food. Dogs very much like them are still with us today. They are the dogs we call Norwegian elkhounds. This breed of dog is a tough, skillful hunter of big animals. And it looks much like a wolf.

73

Another dog of today that hunted big animals long ago is the chow chow. Chow chows have existed in China for at least 2,000 years. They are probably crossbreds of parents from two places very far away from each other. One parent was very likely an early wolflike dog from Siberia or Mongolia, which are north of China. The other parent may have been an early dog from Tibet, a mountainous region that is now in southwestern China.

In a hot country such as Egypt, a very different kind of hunting dog was bred. Because they did not need heavy fur, most became short-haired. These animals lived in broad, flat places where they could see for long distances, so they hunted by sight rather than scent. They had keen eyes, long legs, and slim bodies.

Pictures and carvings made by Egyptian artists of about 5,000 years ago show the kinds of hunting dogs the Egyptians bred. These dogs were slim, elegant-looking animals, with high, pointed ears and pointed muzzles.

Dogs much like them are still with us today. They are the dogs we call the greyhound, the Saluki, the Ibizan hound, and the pharaoh hound. These are among the fastest of all dogs.

Although the very first dogs were probably all hunters, there was soon a need for other kinds of dogs. About 10,000 years ago, people learned how to grow plants and raise goats, sheep, and cattle for food. Now there was a new job for the dog—helping to guard its master's land and herds. So people began to breed guard dogs and herding dogs.

Pictures of large, powerful dogs like today's mastiff have been found in Egyptian drawings from about 5,000 years ago. Roman soldiers probably brought these courageous dogs along as fighting companions when they invaded England more than 2,000 years ago. There, the dogs helped fight off wild animals. And, as areas became more populated, mastiffs became popular as watchdogs, protecting people in their homes.

Greyhound

Cardigan Welsh corgi

When the people called Celts moved into Wales, west of England, about 2,500 years ago, they brought with them the short-legged, pointy-eared dog that came to be called the Cardigan Welsh corgi. At that time the corgi was a valued hunter and watchdog. But in time, the Celts became herders. They then trained the corgi to drive cattle out to pasture and bring them back. The little dogs would nip at the heels of the cattle and then crouch down to avoid the angry kick. After the pastures were fenced in, the corgi almost disappeared. But because enough people loved the dogs, they are still with us.

The Celts also settled in Ireland some 2,500 years ago. And with them came the huge, fierce-looking dogs with gentle hearts that are now called Irish wolfhounds. The

Dogs Through the Ages

wolfhound was used for hunting wolves and giant elk in Ireland for hundreds of years.

Long, long ago, people began to breed very small dogs that they wanted simply as pets and house dogs. The tiny, fluffy, long-haired dog that we call the Maltese was a favorite pet of the ancient Greeks nearly 3,000 years ago. Many Greeks even built special tombs for these dogs. And the tiny Italian greyhound, plainly a small version of the greyhound, was bred by people in what are now Greece and Turkey as a house dog about 2,000 years ago.

Maltese

"New" breeds of dogs

Many breeds of dogs that are very popular today first appeared during the past 1,000 years, so we might call these the "new" breeds of dogs. As with the "old" breeds, people had reasons for developing the newcomers.

About 700 years ago, the otters in the rivers and streams of Europe became a problem for those who fished. Otters eat fish, and the people wanted the fish for themselves. They used the dogs they already had to hunt the otters, but these dogs were not good enough. So, over time, dog breeders developed a big, strong dog with a heavy, waterproof coat and webbed feet—a dog that loved the water and could swim almost as well as an otter. This new breed of dog was called an otterhound.

About 400 years ago, the Germans developed the Great Dane. This dog's ancestry is lost in the mists of time, but it may be a cross between the mastiff and the Irish wolfhound. The Germans bred this giant dog to hunt wild boars, one of the most savage animals in Europe. Why we call this dog a Great Dane is something of a mystery. After all, the Great Dane comes from Germany, not Denmark. We took the name from the French, who at one time called this dog a *grand Danois*,

Dogs Through the Ages

Otterhound

or *Great Danish.* The Germans call this dog *Deutsche Dogge,* which loosely translates as *German mastiff.* But by whatever name, the Great Dane is truly a great dog.

In Russia, where winters are bitterly cold, members of the royal families needed dogs for hunting. The dogs had to be fast and sharp-sighted and able to keep warm in the cold. So, about 400 years ago, the rulers crossed thin-coated greyhoundlike dogs with thick-coated hounds. The swift, hardy dogs that developed were the first borzois, or Russian wolfhounds.

Dogs have long been used to hunt badgers. In Germany, this kind of dog was called a *dachshund.* The name comes from *dachs,* meaning *badger,* and *hund,* meaning *dog.* But it wasn't until about 400 years ago that the breed we call the dachshund first appeared in Germany.

Dachshund

You may think that, with their long bodies and short legs, these dogs look rather strange. But there's a reason for their body shape. The dachshund was bred to squeeze down a badger hole. At first, there were only the smooth and long-haired types. Later, a wire-haired type was bred with a tough coat that protected it from sharp underbrush.

One of the youngest breeds is the Doberman pinscher. These dogs come from Germany. They are named for Louis Dobermann, the original breeder. First bred as a guard dog and watchdog, the courageous Doberman has gained fame as a police dog and war dog.

Another more recent breed is the Chesapeake Bay retriever. In 1807, an English ship was wrecked off the coast of Maryland. All those aboard, including two Newfoundland puppies, were saved. The grateful sailors gave both of the puppies, a male and a female, to their rescuers. The new owners trained the dogs to retrieve ducks. Later, the two dogs were mated with other breeds

Dogs Through the Ages

of dogs, probably retrievers. In time, the breeders developed a dog that could work for hours in the waters of the bay. They called this new breed the Chesapeake Bay retriever.

The Boston terrier breed goes back to about 1870. This dog is a cross between an English bulldog and an English terrier. This "American gentleman among dogs" was once called an American bull terrier. It has since become known as the Boston terrier, after the city where it was bred.

The Black Russian terrier is one of the newest dog breeds. It was only developed after World War II (1939-1945). Breeders in the Soviet Union (now Russia) mixed the rottweiler, giant schnauzer, and Airedale terrier to create a dog that could work in prisons and on military bases.

Chesapeake Bay retriever

Dogs to Remember

83

Greyfriars' Bobby

More than 150 years ago, the great city of Edinburgh in Scotland was a busy, bustling place. The narrow, bumpy streets were filled with horse-drawn carriages, carts, and wagons.

To this city every Wednesday morning, came a farmer named Mr. Grey. And at his side, trotting along on short legs that moved so fast they seemed to twinkle, was Bobby. Bobby was Mr. Grey's Skye terrier—a small, intelligent, short-tailed kind of dog whose bright eyes and stubby legs were nearly covered by his long, flowing hair.

Mr. Grey would spend the morning at market. When the time-gun—a signal cannon that was fired at one o'clock—went off, Mr. Grey and Bobby would head for a small restaurant called Traill's Dining Rooms, which was not far from Greyfriars' Church. There, Mr. Grey and Bobby would have lunch. Lunch was always the same for the little dog—a crisp bun. Mr. Traill, who owned the restaurant, soon came to know the little dog well.

Dogs to Remember

One Wednesday, the farmer and his dog did not appear at the restaurant. Several days passed. Then, one day as the time-gun sounded the hour of one o'clock, Mr. Traill was startled to see a small, thin, bedraggled-looking dog standing in his doorway. It was Bobby, and he was all alone.

"Why, I believe he's hungry," Mr. Traill said to himself. "He's come for a bun, same as always. But where is his master?" He took a bun and held it out to the dog. "Is that it, laddie? Are ye hungry?"

Bobby took the bun, and with the quick, happy sort of skip that a hungry dog often makes when given a bit of food, turned and trotted from the restaurant. Mr. Traill watched him go, wondering what had happened. Was the little dog lost? Had something happened to his master, the farmer Grey?

Sergeant Stubby

Dogs have been helping people in battles and wars for hundreds—if not thousands—of years. In the United States, one such dog, a dog who earned many military and other honors, was a pit bull terrier named Stubby.

Stubby was a scrawny brown and white puppy when he wandered onto the campus of Yale University in New Haven, Connecticut, in 1917. At the time, the 102nd Infantry was training there before being sent to Europe to fight in World War I (1914-1918). Stubby seemed to enjoy running among the men on the practice field as they marched and drilled in preparation for war. One of the men, Private John Robert Conroy, became especially attached to Stubby.

When the 102nd received orders to board a troop ship headed for Europe, Conroy smuggled Stubby aboard. The rest of the men quickly became fond of the little stowaway, and Stubby became the mascot of the 102nd Regiment. The soldiers even taught him to salute—Stubby would raise his right front paw to his face.

Soon after the 102nd arrived in Europe, the regiment was sent to fight in the front lines in France. Stubby had never been trained in the horrific conditions of war, but from the beginning, the small dog reacted calmly to the noise and confusion of the battlefield. When the soldiers heard incoming shells and ran to take cover in the trenches they had dug, Stubby ran, too. Soon, with his superior canine hearing, Stubby would know that shells were coming before the men did. When the soldiers saw Stubby running for the trenches, they would run, too.

But Stubby did more than run and hide from danger. When any of "his" men were injured during a battle, Stubby would run out onto the field, find the soldier, and stay with him until he could be rescued. Stubby himself was wounded in action twice and was sent to a Red Cross hospital where he was taken care of just like a soldier.

Sergeant Stubby displays the medals he was awarded for his service during World War I (1914-1918).

Besides his excellent hearing, Stubby also possessed a canine's superior sense of smell. During a gas attack by the enemy, Stubby gave his troops an early warning and saved the soldiers from certain death. He carried messages across the battlefield, took his turn at guard duty, and once even caught a German spy! For his bravery, Stubby was made an honorary sergeant.

After the war, Sergeant Stubby returned to the United States with Conroy. He was introduced to President Woodrow Wilson (whom Stubby saluted) and also met Presidents Warren G. Harding and Calvin Coolidge. He marched in many parades and was named a life member of the Red Cross, the American Legion, and the YMCA.

When Conroy went to Georgetown University to study law, Stubby became the mascot of the university's football team. He often enjoyed playing with the football on the sidelines at half-time. Stubby eventually died of old age, in 1926, with his favorite soldier, Conroy, at his side.

Barry

The towering, snow-covered Alps form a giant barrier between many of the countries of Europe. For thousands of years, the only way to get over these mountains was to go through the passes. But there were many dangers.

When tired travelers lay down to rest, they often fell asleep. And in the dreadful cold high in the mountains, they could soon freeze to death. Or sudden blizzards might cause them to lose their way. Or huge masses of snow sliding down the mountainside might bury them.

Many hundreds of years ago, a man named Bernard de Menthon built a shelter in one of the passes between Switzerland and Italy. Monks who stayed at the shelter did what they could to help travelers. About 300 years ago, the monks began to use a special sort of dog to go out and search for travelers who were in trouble. By this time, the pass had become known as the Great St. Bernard Pass. So the dogs became known as Saint Bernards.

The Saint Bernards were trained to save lives. They could sniff out people from great distances. They could even find people who were buried under the snow. They would cover freezing people with their large, hairy bodies to warm them. And they would bark with their deep voices to show the monks of the shelter where to come.

The most famous of all these Saint Bernards was named Barry. Barry lived about 200 years ago. Barry helped to save the lives of some 40 people! He once saved a little boy who was trapped on an icy

Dogs to Remember

mountain ledge. The boy was asleep and freezing. Barry covered him with his big, warm body and licked his face to wake him. When the boy awoke, he climbed onto Barry's back. The great Saint Bernard carried him to safety.

There is a story that Barry was killed by a soldier who thought his rescuer was a wolf. But Barry did not die in this sad way. He worked at rescuing people for 10 years. Then the monks sent him to the city of Bern, in Switzerland, where he lived quietly for 4 more years. When he died, his skin was stuffed and mounted. Barry can still be seen in a museum in Bern. Monks kept Saint Bernards at the shelter for more than 300 years, until 2004. During that time, the dogs saved more than 2,500 lives.

The puppy who became a hero

Honey was a 5-month-old cocker spaniel puppy that had just found a home with her new owner, Michael Bosch. Bosch, who was recovering from heart surgery, adopted the puppy from a humane society when her original owner could not take care of her.

Two weeks after the adoption, on a bright fall morning, Bosch and Honey set off in his SUV to run some errands. As Bosch backed down his narrow driveway in the thickly wooded California hills, the sun suddenly blinded him. His car slipped down a steep drop-off, rolling over and over as it fell. Bosch's leg was pinned between the steering wheel, the roof, and the dashboard when a tree branch pierced the roof.

Bosch was terrified. His heart hurt, his ribs hurt, and he couldn't pull his leg free. He quickly checked to see whether Honey was all right. Luckily, she was. Bosch's first thought was to call for help on his cell phone. But the ravine they had fallen into was so deep, the phone would not work. Now he became really scared. Bosch's wife was out of town on a business trip, and his nearest neighbor lived about $\frac{1}{4}$ of a mile away. There was no hope that anyone would know he needed help.

For a long time, Bosch thought about what to do. Then he decided that maybe he could at least save Honey. He carefully pushed the puppy through a broken window

Honey, a cocker spaniel puppy, had only lived with her new owner a few short weeks when she saved Michael Bosch's life.

and told her to go home, not sure if she would even know where home was. After all, she had only lived there for two weeks!

But Honey did not go home. Instead, she ran through the woods until she came to the neighbor's house. She waited outside the door until evening, when the neighbor, Robin, came home from work. Then, Honey pawed at Robin, whimpered, and kept trying to get Robin to follow her. Robin did not understand what Honey wanted, but she knew where the little dog lived and decided to drive her home.

When they reached Bosch's house, Honey ran to the edge of the ravine. She kept pacing back and forth and looking down. Robin did not know what Honey was trying to show her, but suddenly she heard someone yell, "Help!" Bosch had heard the car door slam and had cried out. Robin called 911, and soon a rescue crew arrived in a helicopter.

The rescuers took Bosch to the hospital, where he slowly recovered. They told him that if help had not arrived when it did, he would have died because he had become so weak. Honey had saved his life.

The Colleen Paige Foundation named Honey the National Dog Day Hero Dog of 2006. Honey was honored in a parade in New York City on National Dog Day, August 26.

A race against death

The tiny cabin was one of a few small buildings that looked like dark dots against the snow. Two men peered through the cabin window at the swirling blizzard raging outside. The fury of the wind made the walls rattle.

"Twenty-eight below zero," muttered one of the men. "And that wind's blowin' stronger than ever! She ain't going to let up any."

The other man, a tall, husky giant, nodded.

"What time is it, Charlie?"

Charlie pulled out a battered pocket watch and looked at it. "'Bout a quarter to ten."

The big man turned abruptly away from the window. "Well, I'm going to start, Charlie. No sense in waiting any longer. This blizzard could blow for days." He picked up a sealskin parka and slipped it over his head. It was followed with a second parka made of thick cloth. "Help me hitch up the team."

The two men stepped out of the cabin into the storm-blown night. A big, black dog with one white foreleg came with them. Outside stood a large, rather flimsy-looking wooden sled. And clustered about the sled, lying and sitting in the snow, were 12 more dogs.

Working swiftly, the two men tied the dogs in pairs, forming a "chain" that was hitched to the front of the sled. The big, black dog that had followed them from the cabin was tied by itself at the

Sled driver Gunnar Kaasen hugs Balto, the half wolf, half Siberian husky who led a dog team through a blizzard to save many Alaskans.

94   Dogs to Remember

head of the team. The tall man knelt down beside this dog and stroked its head.

"We've got a tough run to make, Balto," he murmured. "But we can do it, eh boy?"

The big dog looked up at him with bright, intelligent eyes. Balto was the leader of the dog team, picked because he was the smartest and most experienced of all the dogs.

Charlie had stepped back into the cabin. Now he came out again, carrying a large package wrapped in furs. "Here's the stuff, Gunnar."

Gunnar Kaasen took the package and tied it carefully in the sled. Because of what was in this package he was about to risk his life and the lives of all his dogs. He and his team of dogs were going to carry the package some 35 miles (56 kilometers) to the little town of Safety. The journey would take about five hours, through bitter cold and clawing wind. At Safety, another dog team would pick up the package and carry it on to the city of Nome, Alaska. Already, 19 teams, working in relays, had traveled more than 600 miles (966 kilometers) with the package.

The package meant *life* for hundreds of people. An epidemic had struck the city of Nome. The hideous, choking disease called diphtheria was raging in the city. Scores of people had been stricken. Some were already dead. More would die unless the package reached Nome quickly. And, unless the disease was checked, it would spread through the territory, killing thousands!

Only dog teams could get through to Nome. No trains ran in this part of Alaska in 1925. And the airplanes of that time were grounded by the cold. Even if they had been able to get into the air, they could not have flown in such a storm.

So Gunnar Kaasen knew he could not wait for the blizzard to pass. He had to leave now, at once. The package in his sled contained serum with which people could be given shots that would save them from the dreadful disease. He was in a race against death!

Kaasen stepped onto the sled runners that stuck out at the rear. With his gloved hands he gripped the two handles that curved up from the sled's high back. "So long, Charlie," he called. Then, raising his voice against the howl of the wind, he roared, "Mush!"

Mush! It was the signal to the lead dog that meant "go!" And Balto, trained to move the instant he heard that word, leaped forward. The other dogs immediately followed their leader. The sled slid forward, quickly picking up speed as it began to glide smoothly over the snow.

The tiny town of Bluff, from which Kaasen had just set out, was at the edge of the sea. Kaasen guided the sled along the shore. He felt that he would make better time along the flat, open shoreland than he would inland.

The cold wind clawed at him. He could feel its sharpness even through his sealskin parka and pants. The rushing torrent of icy snowflakes stung his cheeks like needles and the moisture of his breath froze in the below-zero cold.

Minutes passed and lengthened into an hour or more. Kaasen was conscious only of the numbing cold and the wind. Because of the swirling snow, he could not see much beyond Balto running at the head of the team. But he knew this trail. He had traveled it many times before. Each familiar landmark that the team passed was just like a signpost guiding the way.

They were making good time and had already reached the Topkok River. The sled's runners hissed over the ice-covered river.

Suddenly Balto stopped. At once the other dogs halted, too. Kaasen hurried forward to see what had happened. To his dismay, he saw that Balto had run into an overflow—a place where water had come up through the ice and had not yet frozen. Balto's paws were wet, and that could mean trouble. His wet feet would stick to the ice as he ran and would soon be torn and bleeding.

Quickly, Kaasen guided the team into a nearby snowdrift. He spent precious minutes carefully drying off Balto's paws.

As soon as the dog was tended to, the man started the team running again. Crossing the river, they started up the side of the great hill that loomed above it. And at the top of Topkok hill Kaasen ran into the full fury of the storm!

Icy snowflakes rushed through the air in a blinding cloud, pushed by the tremendous force of the howling, battering, 80-mile- (130-kilometer-) an-hour wind! The biting, burning cold held Kaasen in a grip that might have frozen the sun.

Desperately, Kaasen squinted ahead into the white-filled darkness. He could no longer even see the wheel dog, the one nearest the sled. It was as if he were alone, floating in the center of a frozen, white cloud. He couldn't tell whether he was still on the trail or not. He couldn't even guess where he was.

Kaasen was faced with a terrible problem. He could no longer guide the team. But he could not stop, and he could not turn back. He could only go on, hoping the dogs could stay on the trail.

"Balto," he muttered to himself. "It's up to you, Balto. You've got to get us there!"

At the front of the team, the big black husky ran steadily over the snow. His jaws were open and his red tongue lolled out of his mouth as he panted with the effort of his run. Perhaps he sensed that his master was no longer guiding the team. But it did not matter. Although as blinded by the blowing snow as the man, Balto did not have to rely on his eyes. He had his nose, his marvelous sense of smell, to keep him on the trail.

Hundreds of dog teams had followed this trail in the past, and Balto could sniff out the scent they had left, even through the packed snow. He was simply following a trail of scent. Now he was truly the leader of the team, leading even his master, who was helpless in the fierce blizzard.

The team sped down the long slope of the hill, across 6 miles (10 kilometers) of flat plain, and over ice-covered Spruce Creek. The dogs had now covered about 13 miles (21 kilometers). Somewhere ahead was the tiny town of Solomon, which lay on the coast, about 33 miles (53 kilometers) from Nome. There was a message for Kaasen in Solomon, a message telling him to wait until the blizzard

Dogs to Remember

was over, telling him that no man or dog could possibly face the terrible fury of the storm.

But Kaasen was not even aware that his team was anywhere near Solomon. He could hardly see his hands on the handles of the sled. And Balto did not know that he should stop at this place. The dog would simply run until his master told him to stop—or until he could run no more. So, in the snow-filled darkness, Kaasen's team raced on past the town.

Now they hit a long stretch of very high, open country. The wind was so fierce that it rocked the sled. More than once the sled tipped over in the loose snow. When this happened, Kaasen would have to make his way down the line of dogs and, working mainly by feel, untangle the harness.

On the team went, led by Balto. Then the trail turned, and the team had the wind at its back. At last they came to the little town of Safety. This was where Kaasen was supposed to turn the package of serum over to the driver of another team. This driver would take it on to Nome. But the cabin was dark. Kaasen was not expected before daylight, so everyone had gone to bed.

Kaasen decided not to stop. He did not want to waste precious time waiting for the other driver to dress and hitch up his team. Nome was only some 21 miles (34 kilometers) away. Kaasen felt that his team could make it. They would make it!

Dog Tracks

The Nose Knows

How was Balto able to follow the trail when neither he nor Gunnar Kaasen could see it? Dogs' noses can pick up, or sense, many more scents than people's noses can. Smell is one of the most highly developed of all of the dog's senses. In fact, a dog's sense of smell is thought to be about 1,000 times sharper than that of a human being. That is because a dog's nose, or muzzle, contains many more *olfactory* (smell) receptors than a human nose. Human beings have only about 5 million olfactory receptors. Different breeds of dogs have varying numbers of such cells. But even a bulldog, with its small snout, has about 100 million olfactory receptors. Labrador retrievers and German shepherds have more than 200 million. That is why such breeds are often used as "sniffer" dogs to find missing people or hidden substances.

A statue of Balto in Central Park in New York City honors all of the sled dogs who carried disease-fighting serum across Alaska during the winter of 1925.

At 5:30 in the morning Kaasen's team reached the snow-covered streets of Nome. In 7 1/2 hours they had covered 53 miles (85 kilometers) in the worst kind of weather. The sled dogs were panting and exhausted. Two of them were half frozen and limping badly. One side of Kaasen's face was frozen. But they had won—they had won the race against death!

After delivering the package of serum, Kaasen staggered up the line of dogs. He fell to his knees beside Balto. Crying softly, he wrapped his arms around the big dog's neck. "Balto," he sobbed. "Damn fine dog! You brought us through!"

Ten months later, Balto, Gunnar Kaasen, and a crowd of several hundred people stood in Central Park in New York City. Many people in New York had raised the money to have a statue made and placed in the park. And now the statue was finished. Today, with speeches and tribute, it would be shown for the first time.

It was a bronze statue of Balto. But this statue was to honor all of the more than 150 dogs that had helped win the race to Nome.

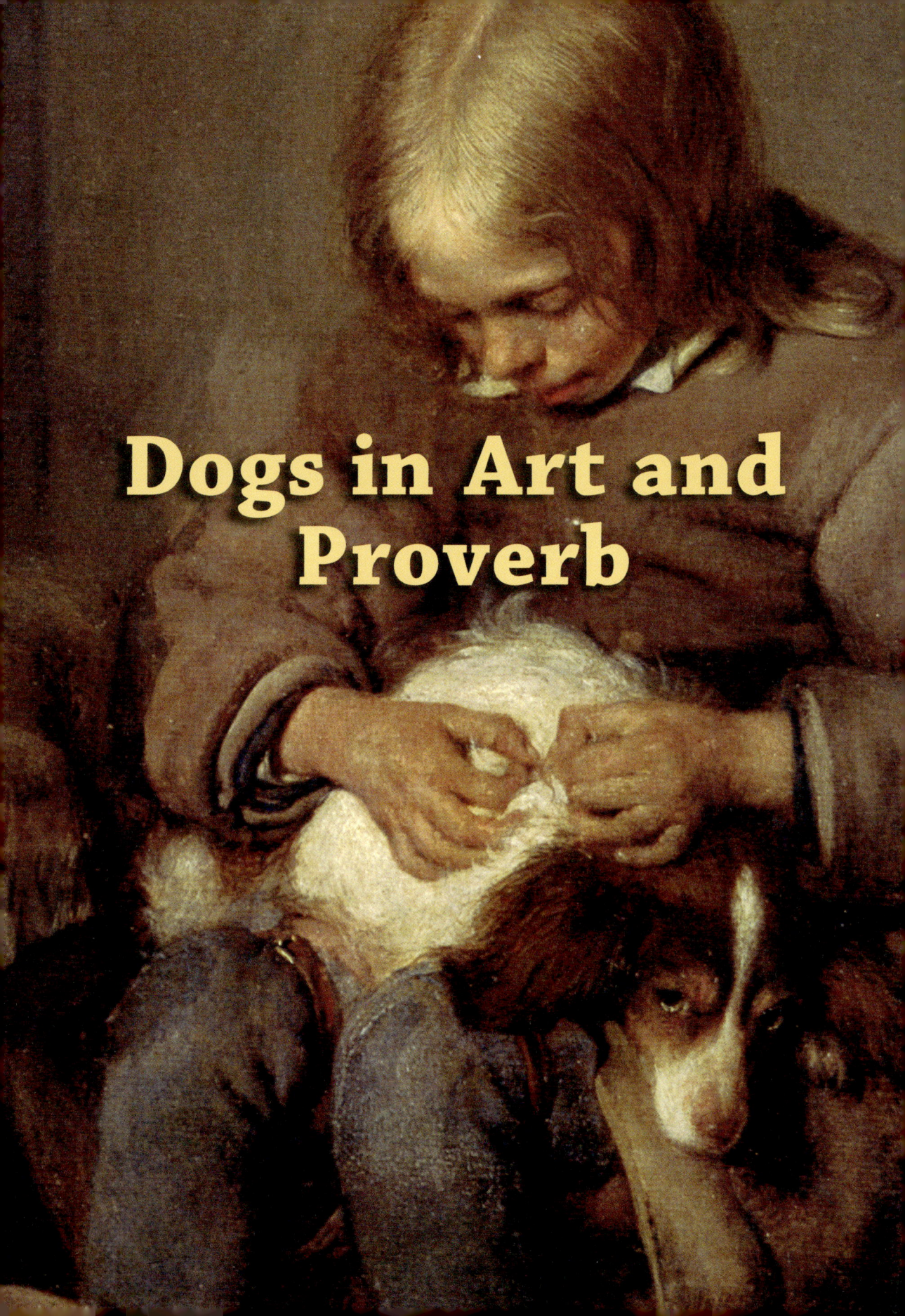

Dogs in Art and Proverb

103

Dogs in art

People have liked dogs for thousands of years. So it isn't surprising that artists in all parts of the world have depicted dogs in works of art since earliest times. The very oldest paintings with dogs in them were made by prehistoric artists as many as 12,000 years ago. These pictures show men and their dogs out hunting.

In ancient Egypt, beginning around 5,000 years ago, artists made bright, exciting paintings of Egyptian kings using dogs to hunt lions and other beasts. The Egyptian artists also made wooden carvings of dogs that look much like the greyhounds and Ibizan hounds of today.

More than 5,000 years ago, in a city called Ur in the country we now know as Iraq, artists made lifelike clay models of dogs that look a lot like today's Saluki.

There are pictures of dogs on many ancient Greek vases. One vase shows two dogs fighting. Another shows two men feasting—and under the table a dog is enjoying its bit of the feast!

A rock art painting made thousands of years ago and discovered in Libya's Sahara desert depicts a man hunting with his dogs.

Dogs in Art and Proverb

In Rome, 2,000 or more years ago, wealthy people often had large pictures called murals painted on the walls of their houses. There were dogs in many of these paintings.

In Europe, during the Middle Ages (from about the 400's through the 1400's), dogs and hunters were a favorite subject for painters and tapestry weavers. Later, when artists were painting pictures of wealthy people, pet dogs were often a part of the picture.

Today, most of the pictures we see of dogs are photographs, though dog owners still enjoy having an artist sketch or paint a portrait of their dog. And it is no longer only wealthy dog owners who are able to have such a work commissioned.

Some artists are showing dogs in different ways—with statues made of welded metal or of wire. And with the development of ever more sophisticated computer software, artists can manipulate dog images on their computers to create endless varieties of digital art.

A statue discovered in an Egyptian tomb by British archaeologists in 1922 depicts an ancient Egyptian god with the head of a jackal. Jackals are wild dogs that still live in Africa, Asia, and southeastern Europe.

Why is the dog so shiny on this bronze plaque? The plaque is part of the base of a statue of St. John Nepomuk erected in the Czech city of Prague in 1683. Many people believe that rubbing the dog will bring good luck. As you can see, the dog has been petted a lot over the last 325 years!

Dogs in Art and Proverb

Spaniels rest at the feet of the children of British King Charles I in a portrait painted in 1637 (below). This particular kind of spaniel came to be called the Cavalier King Charles spaniel, because the dogs were such favorites of the king.

German artist Franz Marc painted his own dog, Russi, a white Siberian shepherd, lying in the snow (left) in about 1910.

109

The proverbial dog

All over the world, people have old sayings that offer good advice. Such sayings are called *proverbs*. In many proverbs, dogs, and their habits, are used to make a point.

Did anyone ever tell you to "Let sleeping dogs lie"? This is just another way of saying, "Leave well enough alone" or "Don't mess around with something that's all right as it is." This saying probably comes from the idea that if you wake a sleeping dog, it might be startled and bite you.

Another old saying is, "If you lie down with dogs, you'll get up with fleas." Dogs used to get fleas much more often in the past, when they spent a lot of time outside. And fleas jump easily from one person or animal to another. The saying means that if you spend a lot of time with people who have bad habits or bad ways, you'll soon pick up those bad behaviors yourself.

People often say, "You can't teach an old dog new tricks." This means that it's hard to get someone to change old habits.

There is an old Danish proverb that says, "The dog's kennel is not the place to keep a sausage." This means that you shouldn't put something that's important to you in a place where others might be tempted to take it.

Have you ever heard someone say, "Barking dogs never bite," or "Every dog has his day," or "A good dog deserves a good bone"? Can you figure out what these proverbs mean?

Dogs in Art and Proverb

Dog talk

Have you ever read a book that had "dog-eared" pages? Were you ever "sick as a dog" or "dog-tired"? Dogs are so much a part of our lives that our language is filled with expressions such as these.

A "dog-eared" page is one that has a folded corner, so that it looks like the floppy ear of a dog. And if you are "sick as a dog," you are *very* sick. When you feel "dog-tired," you may have been exercising or working hard and want to curl up like a dog and go to sleep.

You might hear a friend say that she did something her parents did not like, so she is "in the doghouse." Your friend means that she feels like a dog who has been put away in its doghouse for doing something wrong. If your friend is acting like he has "his tail between his legs," it means that he is ashamed of something he has done. On the other hand, if someone is "as pleased as a dog with two tails," that person is very, very happy.

People will sometimes say that "the tail is wagging the dog." They mean that the least important person in a group has taken over or that some minor point has become so blown out of proportion that it has changed the meaning of an important rule or policy.

When two dogs fight, they often circle one another before one of them attacks the other. During World War I and World War II, enemy airplanes circled and dove at one another in much the same way. And so, even though battles between fighter planes have changed, an air battle is still called a "dogfight."

Working Dogs and Show Dogs

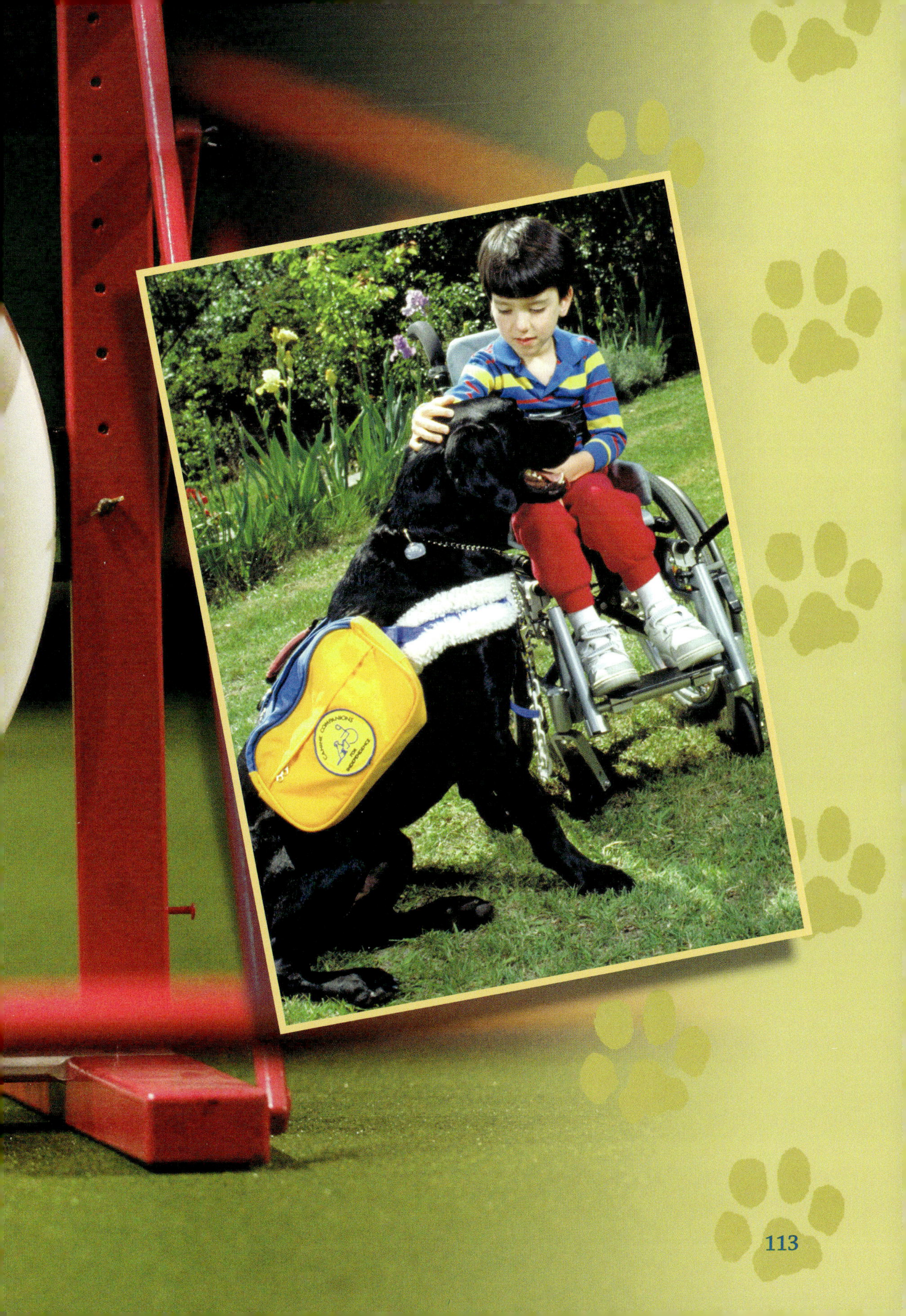

Extra-special dogs

If you love dogs, all dogs are special. But some dogs work at jobs that make them extra special. These dogs are more than companions or protectors. Called *assistance dogs,* they help people who have physical or other disabilities. *Guide dogs,* or *seeing eye dogs,* help those who cannot see. *Signal dogs,* or *hearing ear dogs,* help those who cannot hear. *Service dogs* help those who are unable to do physical activities, such as walk or use their hands. *Special needs dogs* help those with other kinds of problems, such as memory loss or seizures.

Guide dogs

Guide dogs usually are purebreds. The first kind of dog trained for this important work was the German shepherd. Today, many breeds are trained as guide dogs. You may see a Labrador retriever, golden retriever, or German shepherd guiding someone who is blind. Signal dogs tend to be mixed breeds, small to medium in size.

A guide dog must be smart, gentle, and easy to groom. As a rule, a smart dog learns quickly and is easy to train. How does a dog become a guide dog? There are several groups that train guide dogs. Some breed their own dogs, some accept dogs as gifts, some buy dogs, and some get dogs in all these ways.

Each of the many different guide dog groups has slightly different training methods. Here is what happens at one school where purebred dogs are trained as guide dogs.

When a puppy is about 7 weeks old, it is given a number of tests to see if it is likely to make a good guide dog. How does it react to a collar and leash? Does it tend to come when called? Is it startled if someone jumps in front of it? How does it react to walking on different kinds of surfaces? Is it willing to try going up and down stairs? Does it show a desire to fetch things?

Working Dogs and Show Dogs

There are good reasons for these and other tests of this kind. If the puppy is willing to come when called, it is likely to respond willingly to actual training. If the puppy is not frightened by sudden movement or by walking on a strange surface, it is not likely to jump or run when it is faced with a strange situation on the street. And if the puppy wants to retrieve, it should not be too difficult to teach it to fetch whatever has been dropped.

A guide dog waits until it is safe to help its owner across the street. Guide dogs are trained to recognize danger and learn how to lead their owners around or through it.

If the puppy passes these tests, it is ready for the next step. At about 12 weeks of age, the pup goes to live with a carefully selected family. During the next nine months, the dog will learn what life is like outside the kennel. It will have a chance to get used to the many strange sights and sounds of the world.

When it is about 4 months old, the puppy starts attending obedience school. Now it will learn to respond to such commands as *come, forward, sit, stand, down,* and *stay.* It will also learn to *heel* (keep close behind a person) on and off a leash, to stay in position during left and right turns, and to retrieve on command.

At about 1 year of age, the dog is returned to the kennel. There, a trainer begins the real task of training the dog for its life's work. This training takes from four to six months. After a review of all the basic commands, the dog is fitted with a harness that has a U-shaped handle. The dog will wear the harness for most of its life.

Holding the handle and leash, the trainer puts the dog through every kind of experience it will have with a person whose vision is impaired. The trainer takes the guide dog into all kinds of crowded places—on the street, in stores, in restaurants and public buildings. The dog and its trainer walk up and down stairs and go up and down in elevators. They go through regular doors and revolving doors. The dog is taught to stop at a curb, as a warning that the handler must step up or down. And the dog learns to be alert for things it can safely walk under but the trainer can't.

A guide dog becomes familiar with a busy airport security checkpoint. Trainers try to put the dogs through a variety of situations so that the dogs are comfortable in similar places once they begin working.

The guide dog also learns to wait for traffic to stop before crossing a street. If the trainer commands the dog to do something that might be dangerous, such as crossing when a car is turning a corner, the guide dog is taught to disobey. It learns to wait until it is safe. Then the dog moves forward, leading the trainer, who is guided by the movement of the U-shaped handle.

In the last days of training, the trainer is blindfolded. Then it is

Working Dogs and Show Dogs

completely up to the guide dog to see that all goes safely.

Now the guide dog is ready to meet the person whom it will actually be living with and helping. Both the dog and the new owner will go through four weeks of training under the watchful eye of the trainer. After the dog and the person become used to working together, they go home and begin their new life.

Signal dogs

Like guide dogs, signal dogs are carefully trained to help their owner. However, signal dogs are trained to alert their handler to everyday sounds—a doorbell, a telephone ring, an alarm clock, a microwave bell, or a smoke alarm.

Teaching a dog to respond to a sound takes a lot of time and practice. For example, to teach a dog to respond to an alarm clock, one trainer lies in bed while another holds the dog on a leash. When the alarm sounds, the trainer leads the dog to the bed and coaxes the animal to nudge and awaken the sleeping person. When the dog does this successfully, it is hugged and praised. This action is repeated until, without the trainer's help, the dog awakens the person when the alarm sounds. In the same way, the dog is taught to respond to a doorbell, a smoke alarm, or other important sounds that the owner cannot hear.

Training for a signal dog takes about three to six months. The dog is then presented to the new owner. If the person has other special needs, the dog receives further training at this time. For instance, if the owner has a baby, the dog will learn to respond when the baby cries.

Service dogs

Service dogs, or mobility assist dogs, take the place of arms and legs for a person who doesn't have them or can't use them. Service dogs pull people in wheelchairs and help people balance on crutches. With a backpack on their backs,

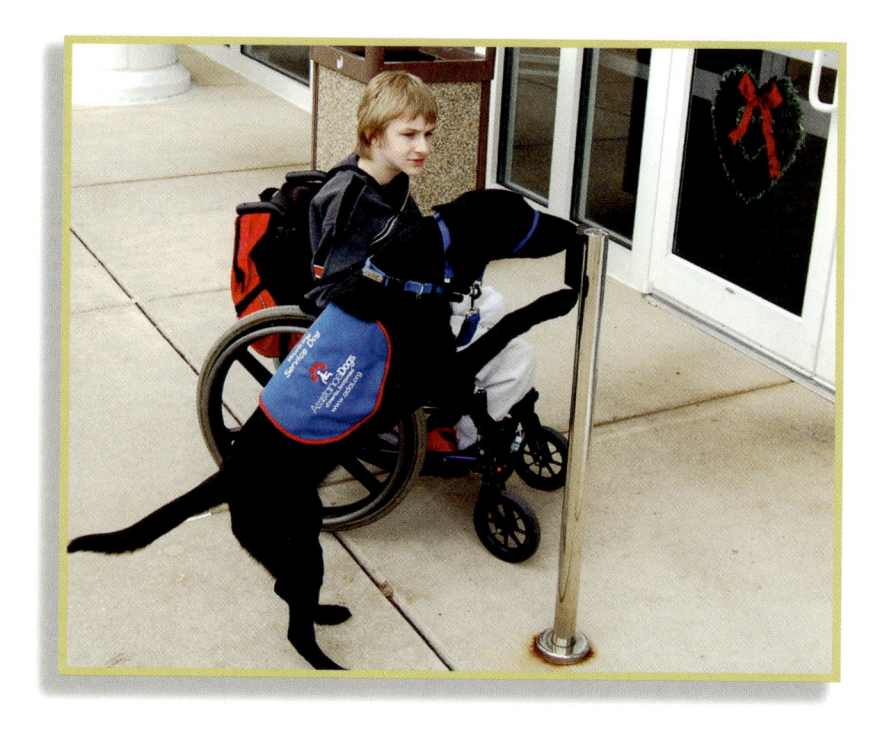

A service dog presses the mechanism that will open the door for its owner. Such dogs are trained to perform the specific tasks their owners need help with.

these dogs carry groceries, books, laptop computers, and other things for their owners. They are also trained to retrieve objects their owners can't reach or have dropped, help their owners dress and undress, and turn lights on and off. Many purebreds and even some mutts from animal shelters make good service dogs, but the most popular breeds are golden retrievers and Labrador retrievers.

Special needs dogs

Special needs dogs are trained to help their owners with a variety of physical, mental, and emotional needs. For example, an older person living alone may own a special needs dog just to keep him or her from being lonely and to help with simple tasks around the house. Or a child with epilepsy may have a *seizure alert dog* that is trained to help the child during an epileptic seizure and go for help. A special needs dog may

Working Dogs and Show Dogs

also be trained to help a person with memory problems or emotional problems.

Some dogs are especially good at visiting people and cheering them up. These dogs are called *therapy dogs*. Assistance dogs belong to only one person and help only that person. But while therapy dogs have one trainer-owner, they help many people, and therapy dogs help different people at different times. For example, an owner of a therapy dog may take the dog to a hospital to visit three or four patients. Then, the owner may take the dog to a nursing home to visit a group of older people. And sometimes, the dog may be taken to visit prisoners in jail. Therapy dogs don't need as much training as do assistance dogs. With very little training, any dog that is smart, likes to be with people, and can stay calm in any situation can become a therapy dog.

Most assistance dogs live with their owner for many years. When the dog is ready to retire, it returns to the training school and another dog is trained as a replacement. What happens to the "old" dog? People at the school find it a good home, where the dog can spend its days taking it easy.

The next time you see an assistance dog in action, watch the way the dog works. You will soon know that you are watching a dog that is extra special!

A therapy dog visits a resident in a retirement community. Therapy dogs must enjoy being with people and be able to remain calm in any situation.

Crime fighters

Every morning, in families everywhere, mothers and fathers get ready to go to work, and children get ready to go to school. But in some families, the family dog gets ready to go to work, too! Such a dog is a police dog, and it lives with the police officer's family.

You may see police officers and their dogs patrolling in a park, at a beach, or at an elevated-train station. By being in these places, they might prevent a crime.

Police forces in all parts of the world use trained dogs to help with police work. Police dogs can do many things that a police officer cannot do. They can go into pitch-dark places and, with their keen noses, quickly lead the officer to where a criminal is hiding.

Dogs can run much faster than people, so they can catch a criminal who is running away. The dogs are trained to corner a suspect,

A police dog watches attentively as commuters come and go in New York City's Grand Central Station.

Working Dogs and Show Dogs

or to grab an arm or leg and hold on, until an officer can make the arrest. Police dogs can track down criminals, search out hidden evidence, and find lost children or injured people. Some of the dogs are trained to sniff out drugs and explosives.

It takes a lot of training to turn a dog into a police dog. And not just any dog can be used for this work. Most police dogs are German shepherds. These dogs are smart, strong, brave, and big enough to either gently help a small child or terrify a desperate criminal. But other breeds, including the Airedale terrier, bloodhound, boxer, Doberman pinscher, golden retriever, and Labrador retriever are often used for police work.

A bomb detection dog sniffs for explosives in passengers' luggage at an airport.

A police dog's training usually begins when the dog is about a year old. The dog must pass tests to make sure that it is healthy, intelligent, and neither shy nor savage. Then the training starts. The dog and the police officer who will be its master are trained together. The dog learns to obey only its master. It is taught to climb ladders, go through windows, crawl into tight places, and not to fear fire. The dog also learns to catch criminals without hurting them, to search for things, and to alert its master by barking when it finds what it is searching for.

When the training is over, the dog and the police officer become partners. They have learned to love and trust each other. From then on, the dog lives at the officer's home and is one of the family.

A bloodhound tries to pick up the scent of a lost child on a mountain trail in Colorado. Bloodhounds have a keen sense of smell and are often used to track people who are lost or missing.

On the trail

The best-known detective of the dog world is probably the big, sad-looking dog with the wrinkled face and the exceptional sense of smell. What dog is it? With these clues, you probably know the dog is the bloodhound. *Bloodhound* seems a strange name for such a gentle dog. Some people say that the name is short for *blooded hound*. *Blooded* is a term used for animals that come from good stock. And the bloodhound has been a purebred dog for about 1,000 years.

Some books and movies have given people the wrong idea about bloodhounds. Bloodhounds are often depicted searching in howling packs. But in real life, bloodhounds are almost always worked alone or, at most, in pairs. The bloodhound does not yelp and howl when on the scent. It usually tracks quietly. And it will go on for as long as it can find the scent. In fact, one dog followed a trail for 138 miles (222 kilometers)—and found the person! Another

Working Dogs and Show Dogs

A German shepherd searches World Trade Center rubble for survivors of the terrorist attack in New York City on Sept. 11, 2001.

dog successfully followed a trail that was four-and-a-half days old.

When a bloodhound finds someone, it never attacks. It wags its tail! It is happy to find the person it was looking for. To the dog, there is no difference between a lost child and a criminal.

But the bloodhound is not the only breed that makes a great search-and-rescue dog. German shepherds, golden retrievers, and Labrador retrievers are all wonderful trackers. Newfoundlands, with their love of the water, their thick coats, and their strong muscles, are excellent water rescue dogs. They have been known to save children who have fallen into the water and to carry lifelines to boats that have been shipwrecked.

Some search-and-rescue dogs begin their training as puppies. Others are older when they begin training. Such dogs learn many of the skills that police dogs learn. But their most important training is in tracking the scent of a person. Search-and-rescue dogs learn to separate one person's scent from another's and can even pick up a scent that is carried on the wind.

Sheepdogs and cattle dogs

Many thousands of years ago, people began to breed and train dogs to help care for herds of sheep and cattle. And many kinds of dogs have had such jobs ever since.

For a long time, dogs that looked after flocks of sheep had to be both shepherds and warriors. They had to be big, fierce animals that could fight off wolves that might attack the sheep. But today, wolves are gone from most parts of the world. Sheepdogs are now bred for intelligence, speed, and the ability to work for long hours.

Sheepdogs are smart. To turn back a stray sheep, the dog chases after it, crouches before it, and glares at the sheep until it turns back to the flock. A good dog can even separate a particular sheep from the rest of the flock.

A sheepdog has to be able to work for hours and is almost always on the move. When it takes a flock somewhere, the dog has to run back and forth around the sheep to keep them together and moving

A border collie (below) stares down a flock of sheep to prevent them from moving in the wrong direction. A herding dog (opposite page) directs a stray calf back to the herd.

Working Dogs and Show Dogs

in the direction it wants them to go. This means that the dog will travel many more times the actual distance the flock is moved.

The dog most widely used for herding sheep today is the small, smart, tough border collie. But in Australia, where a lot of sheep are raised, the Australian shepherd is also a favorite.

In the past, many kinds of dogs were bred for this work. Sometimes you can tell by the breed name which dogs were once sheepdogs and the country in which the breed was first developed. The German shepherd, the Old English sheepdog, and the Belgian sheepdog all once helped care for flocks of sheep. The collie, bred in Scotland, and the puli and komondor, bred in Hungary, were sheepdogs, too.

Cattle dogs don't work quite the same way as sheepdogs. A cattle dog nips at the heels of cattle to make the animals do what is wanted. A cattle dog learns to spot which hind leg bears the animal's weight. The dog nips at that heel. The dog then has time to crouch down before the animal can shift its weight and kick.

Dogs bred to herd cattle include the Cardigan Welsh corgi, the Pembroke Welsh corgi, the rottweiler, and the Australian cattle dog.

Acrobats and actors

A small dog displays its jump-roping skills during a performance with the Kelly Miller Circus.

As the band plays, a woman in a sparkly costume and a young boy run out into the ring. They are carrying a jump rope and start to turn it. The crowd waits quietly to see what will happen next. This is supposed to be a circus, and watching people twirling a rope is not very exciting. But suddenly a small dog runs out into the ring. He waits for just the right moment and begins to jump rope. The crowd's laughter turns into ooh's and ah's as the tiny acrobat leaps into the air over and over again, never missing a beat.

There are performing dogs all over the world. You've probably seen dog acts in the circus, in the movies, or on television.

It takes a lot of training to turn a dog into an acrobat or an actor. And, as any dog trainer will tell you, it also takes a lot of love and patience. Acting in front of a camera is especially difficult. Because of the microphones, the trainer cannot give the dog voice commands. So the dog has to be trained to obey hand signals. And the trainer has to

Working Dogs and Show Dogs

work behind the cameras, or off to the side, to stay out of the picture.

Many individual dogs have become movie and television stars. Perhaps the most famous one of all time was Lassie. Through the years there have been many Lassies, all of them—except for the star of the 2006 film *Lassie*—directly related to the first. And, strange as it may seem, since *lassie* is a Scottish term for a young girl, each Lassie has been a male!

The first Lassie was a collie named Pal. One day, Pal's owner brought his dog to the training school run by Rudd Weatherwax, one of the best dog trainers in Hollywood. The owner wanted the trainer to break Pal of the habits of chasing motorcycles and barking all the time. Pal's owner ended up giving the dog to Weatherwax because he could not pay for the training. Rudd Weatherwax continued to train the dog. Pal became such a good actor, he won the part of Lassie in the movie *Lassie Come-Home* (1943). After that, there were several Lassie movies, and the

The most famous collie in the world, Lassie, appeared in its first movie, **Lassie Come-Home** (1943), with Elizabeth Taylor (below).

127

many Lassies became television stars, too. The original Lassie television series, which first aired in 1954, was one of the longest-running series in history.

One of the first dogs to become a great movie star was a German shepherd by the name of Rin-Tin-Tin. Believe it or not, this dog was found in a German trench during World War I. Corporal Lee Duncan, the American soldier who found the puppy, named the dog after a small woolen doll that French girls gave to soldiers as good luck charms. He brought the dog home to the United States and trained it himself.

Rin-Tin-Tin made many movies. In fact, he became so popular, he helped make the German shepherd dog a favorite pet.

A small, shaggy mongrel named Benji also won fame as an actor. Benji had a successful television career in the 1960's. Then he became a movie star in more than one big hit, including *Benji* (1973) and *Benji the Hunted* (1987).

During the 1990's and early 2000's, several films chronicled the adventures—and misadventures—of a lovable Saint Bernard and his family. The films followed the dog, Beethoven, who was played by several Saint Bernards, from puppyhood in *Beethoven* (1992) through fatherhood in *Beethoven's 2nd* (1993), obedience school in *Beethoven's 4th* (2001), and beyond.

A golden retriever named Buddy became a movie star in the late 1990's as a sports hero. Buddy could master any sport. In movies and

German shepherd Rin-Tin-Tin, a movie star of the 1920's, was found in a German trench during World War I by an American soldier.

Working Dogs and Show Dogs

videos, he played baseball, basketball, football, soccer, and volleyball. His movie titles include *Air Bud: Golden Receiver* (1998) and *Air Bud: World Pup* (2000).

Wherever they appear, performing dogs are always entertainment favorites.

Beethoven (right), a Saint Bernard, involved his movie family in many adventures in a series of films that began in the 1990's. Golden retriever Buddy (below) played several different sports in movies of the 1990's and 2000's.

129

Choosing champion dogs

A neighborhood dog show can be a lot of fun. Boys and girls spend hours grooming their pets and having them practice tricks. There may be prizes for the smartest dog, biggest dog, littlest dog, and so on. It's all in fun, and it makes no difference if the dogs are purebreds or mongrels.

But a real dog show, the kind organized by dog clubs, is a serious affair. The dogs in these shows must be purebreds. And the judges are people who really know about dogs.

In the United States, most dog shows are run under the rules of the American Kennel Club (AKC). There are three kinds of shows. One is the specialty show, which is limited to dogs of one breed. Another is the group show, for dogs that belong to one group of breeds, such as the Herding Group or the Terrier Group. The third kind of show is called an all-breed show, in which any recognized breed of dog can be entered. You may also hear the term **benched show.** At a benched show, the dogs must be present for the entire show. When not being judged, the dogs are displayed on benches in individual stalls. This gives people a chance to see the dogs.

Conformation shows

A dog show, or conformation show as it is usually called, is something of a beauty contest. The dogs are judged on how well they conform, or match up, to the different standards set for each breed. The judges rate each dog on such points as color, coat, teeth, shape and size of body, right down to the way the dog carries its tail and how well it stands, walks, and trots. A dog can earn from 1 to 5 points at a show. It takes 15 points, including two major shows under two different judges, to become a **Champion.**

The dogs are judged in steps. At the first step, there are six classes for the males (called **dogs**) and six classes for the females (called **bitches**) of each breed. The winner of each class gets a blue ribbon and goes on to the next step. At the second step, the best of the six males is named "Winners Dog" and the best of the six females is named "Winners Bitch." These two get points toward their championships. At the third step, the Winners Dog and Winners Bitch compete against each other and any champions of that breed entered in the show. This winner is named "Best of Breed" and gets more points added to its score.

A proud dog and its owners display the trophy they won in a local dog show. Dogs don't have to be purebreds at local shows, and the rules are often less strict.

If the show is an all-breed show, the breeds in each of the seven AKC groups—Sporting Dogs, Hounds, Working Dogs, Herding Dogs, Terriers, Toys, and Nonsporting Dogs—are judged. One dog is picked as the best in each group. These dogs are then judged and the winner of this final step is the dog that is "Best in Show."

One of the most important dog shows in the United States is the Westminster Kennel Club Show, held once a year in

New York City. In the United Kingdom, the most important dog show is Crufts, held yearly in Birmingham, England.

Dog shows are more than *just* beauty contests. Dog shows help people to improve the quality of each breed. Many winners and champions are picked for mating because there is a good chance their offspring will be fine puppies. And, of course, dog shows help to interest people in the different breeds of dogs.

If you're ever lucky enough to own a puppy whose mother or father was a champion, you can be sure you have a fine dog. Perhaps your dog will become a champion, too.

An English springer spaniel is shown off by its handler (left) in the Westminster Dog Show. Handlers prepare their champion purebreds (below) to be judged at Westminster.

Working Dogs and Show Dogs

An Irish setter shows off its broad jump at an obedience trial.

Degrees for dogs

It's exciting to watch a smart, well-behaved dog following commands. That's what an obedience trial is all about. You can usually see obedience trials at dog shows.

In an obedience trial, dogs do a number of things to show how well-trained and obedient they are. Dogs that pass these trials are given degrees, or titles. If you'd like to enter your dog in an obedience trial, here is what your dog must be able to do.

The first title is Novice, or Companion Dog (CD). There are six tests your dog has to pass to earn this title. Your dog must heel on and off a leash. It must stand quietly for a physical examination and come when called. And it must first sit for one minute and then lie down for three minutes with you in sight.

Dogs that earn the Companion Dog title may try for the Open level, or Companion Dog Excellent (CDX). To win this title, your dog must heel off-leash at different speeds and make a figure eight. It must again come when called, but while coming, *drop* (lie down) instantly on command. It has to make an ordinary retrieve and a retrieve that

Dog Tracks

Pleased to Meet You

It's fun to see all kinds of dogs at dog shows or trials, and you may want to pet some of them. Here are a few hints that the American Kennel Club suggests to make the experience as fun for the dog as it is for you:

1. Always approach a strange dog slowly.
2. Ask the dog's owner whether it is all right to pet it.
3. If the owner says yes, make a fist with the back of your hand facing upward.
4. Slowly extend it to the dog so that it can sniff you and learn your scent.
5. After the dog has sniffed you, pet it gently under the chin or on the chest.

includes jumping over a high fence. It also has to make a broad jump over several low obstacles set close together. Finally, it must sit for three minutes and then lie down for five minutes while you are out of sight.

An obedient dog is a better companion and pet than one that does as it pleases. Your dog should come at once when you call, it should heel at your left side, and it should sit or lie down quietly when you want it to. Dogs are easily taught to do these things. But they must be taught.

Many dog clubs hold obedience training classes for dogs. All kinds of dogs, both purebreds and crossbreds, are welcome. Usually, the dogs learn one "lesson" a week and go to school for six or eight weeks. If you want to have a well-trained dog, one that will obey you instantly, obedience classes can be a big help. Still, most of the work of training your dog must come from you, the owner.

Trials and tests for working dogs

At a dog show, purebred dogs of all kinds are judged on their looks. At an obedience trial, dogs are judged on how well they obey commands. But other kinds of tests and trials are only for specific kinds of purebred dogs.

A field trial, for example, is for purebred hunting dogs. The dogs are judged on how well they work. There are different kinds of trials for each of the different breeds.

Beagles, basset hounds, and dachshunds usually compete in pairs. Their job is to find and trail rabbits. Pointers and setters hunt for hidden birds. These dogs also work in pairs. They are judged on their air of eagerness, on the way they point when they find a bird, and their steadiness while the hunter is shooting.

Spaniels have to find and flush birds. The moment the bird flies up, the dog must drop to the ground while the hunter shoots. The dog then watches alertly to see where the bird falls and upon command, retrieves the bird.

Retrievers are tested on land and in the water. In a water trial, the dogs may have to make three retrieves in a single test. Live, dead, or dummy ducks may be used. As the dog watches, three shots are

An English pointer signals that it has found a bird by standing absolutely still with its nose pointing in the bird's direction.

A Labrador retriever successfully returns a duck decoy to its handler.

fired into the air, and three ducks are tossed into the water. On command, the retriever must leap into the water, swim to a duck, and bring it back unharmed. The dog must then retrieve the other two ducks, one at a time.

Another test is called a blind retrieve. A dead duck is hidden, perhaps on an island in a lake. The dog has not seen the bird fall and does not know where it is. The dog's master points toward the island and commands, "Fetch!" The dog must follow its master's signals until it is close enough to the bird to smell it. Then it must make a speedy retrieve. A dog that does well in field trials can win the title of Field Champion.

Herding dogs

Herding dogs have their own trials. Any purebred dog in the Herding Group—such as a collie, corgi, German shepherd, or sheepdog—can participate. Samoyeds and rottweilers of the Working Group are also eligible.

At these events, the dogs and their owners show how well they can work together, managing such livestock as sheep, cattle, goats, or ducks. The dogs are trained to respond to voice commands, whistles, and hand signals.

There are four groups in which herding dogs can be tested. Shepherds have to show that they can lead a flock, usually of sheep. Drovers move a flock—usually of either sheep or cattle—from behind. Livestock Guarders must protect a flock from predators. And All-Round Farm Dogs have to be good at many different tasks.

Testing

In each group, there are several levels that the dogs can achieve. The simplest test is to see whether an untrained dog has the instincts to work as a herding dog. Such a dog earns the title Herding Tested Dog. The highest level is Herding Champion. To win the title Herding Champion, a dog has to be able to herd even the most difficult livestock under a variety of conditions. And all of the tests have to be completed within a time limit.

Another kind of test is called *coursing,* or *sight hunting.* Only purebred sighthounds can participate in this event. Sighthounds were used in ancient times to hunt fast-footed prey over open fields. They follow their prey by sight rather than smell. Sighthounds include greyhounds, Irish wolfhounds, Rhodesian ridgebacks, Salukis, and whippets.

During a coursing trial, an artificial lure, such as a fluttering plastic bag, is pulled across an open field quickly along a series of wires. The dogs are tested in groups of two's or three's. When the lure begins to move, the handlers release the dogs, and the dogs give chase! They can reach incredible speeds as they follow the lure across the field. The dogs earn points for speed, endurance, and ability. They lose points if they decide to play with each other instead of run! In this type of trial, a dog can earn the title Master Courser.

Let it snow!

When heavy snows begin to fall, it's time for the thrilling winter sport of sled-dog racing. Each year in the United States, from Alaska to New Hampshire and across the Upper Midwest, and in Canada and Europe there are hundreds of exciting sled-dog races. The most famous of these races—called the Iditarod *(eye DIHT uh rahd)*—takes place in Alaska.

As many as 2,000 dogs—mostly Siberian huskies, Alaskan malamutes, and Samoyeds—may be entered in one of these events. In most races there are 3 to 10 dogs on a team. In the Iditarod, the teams have from 12 to 16 dogs. The dogs are hitched in pairs, sometimes with a single lead dog at the head of the team. The lead dogs are all-important, because the drivers have no reins. They must control their teams by shouted commands.

A contest of speed

A sled-dog race is a speed contest. The teams start off one at a time, racing against the clock. The dogs have to pull a driver and sled over a trail that may be anywhere from 10 to 30 miles (16 to 80 kilometers) long. A good team will average about 20 miles (30 kilometers) per hour. The Iditarod covers about 1,000 miles (1,770 kilometers). It usually lasts 9 to 12 days but may sometimes last as much as 2 weeks or more.

At the shout of "Hike!" a team races off down the narrow trail. Soon, a red flag on the right warns of a right turn. The driver shouts "Gee!" and the team swings right. On they go, the dogs enjoying the race as much as the spectators. The driver spots a red flag on the left and a shout of "Haw!" turns the team to the left.

A driver and his team approach a checkpoint during the Iditarod, one of the most famous sled-dog races, which covers about 1,000 miles (1,770 kilometers) across Alaska.

The finish line is just ahead. Now the driver snaps his short whip to get the dogs to go faster. He may snap the whip, but he is not allowed to whip the dogs. As the sled crosses the finish line, a shout of "Whoa!" brings the team to a halt. The driver has done well, but he won't know exactly how well until the winning time is announced.

At least he has been lucky in one way. All of his dogs have finished in harness. Not one has pulled a muscle or come up lame. A driver must finish a race with all the dogs he starts with, even if it means carrying a dog on the sled.

Dogs in Myth and Legend

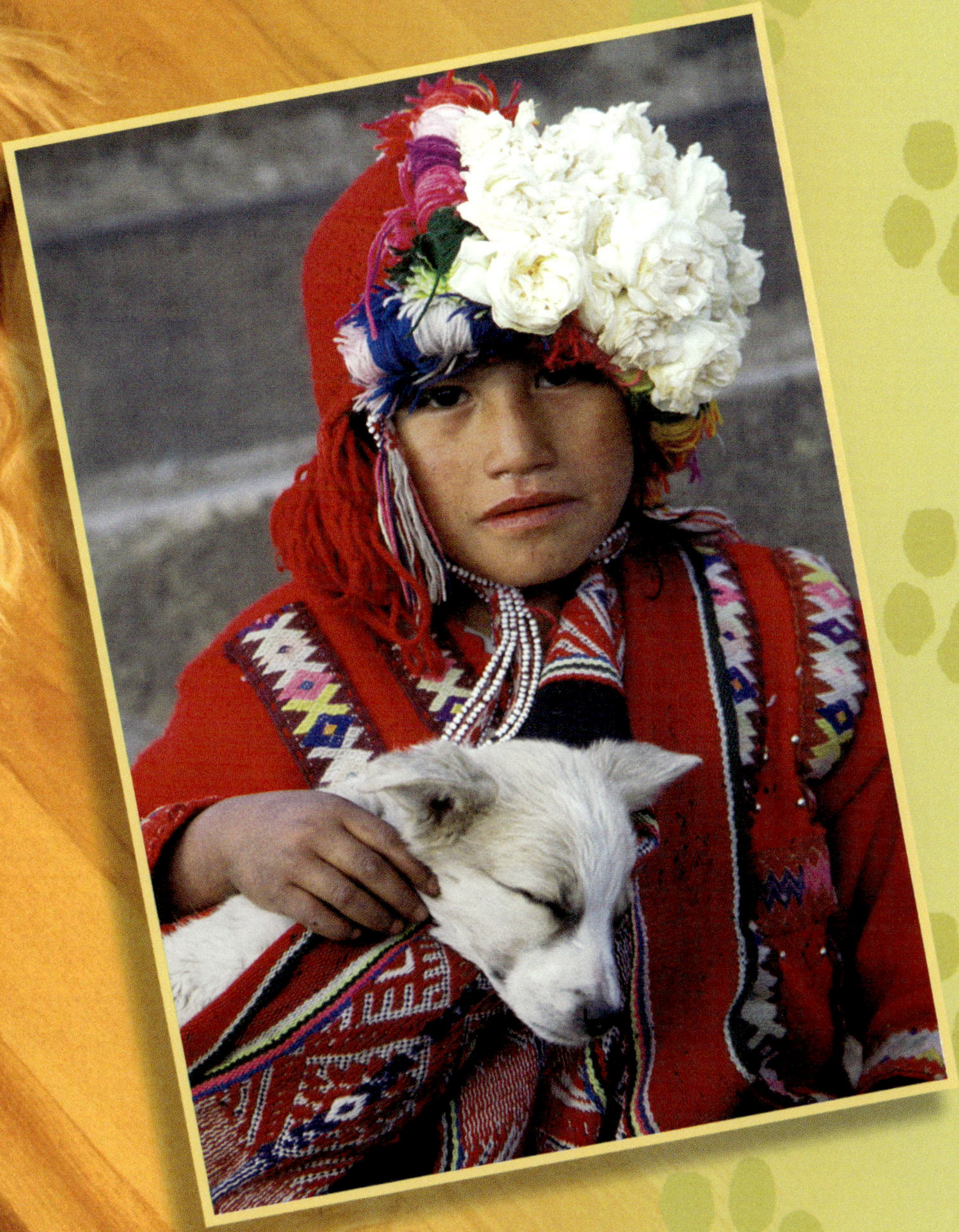

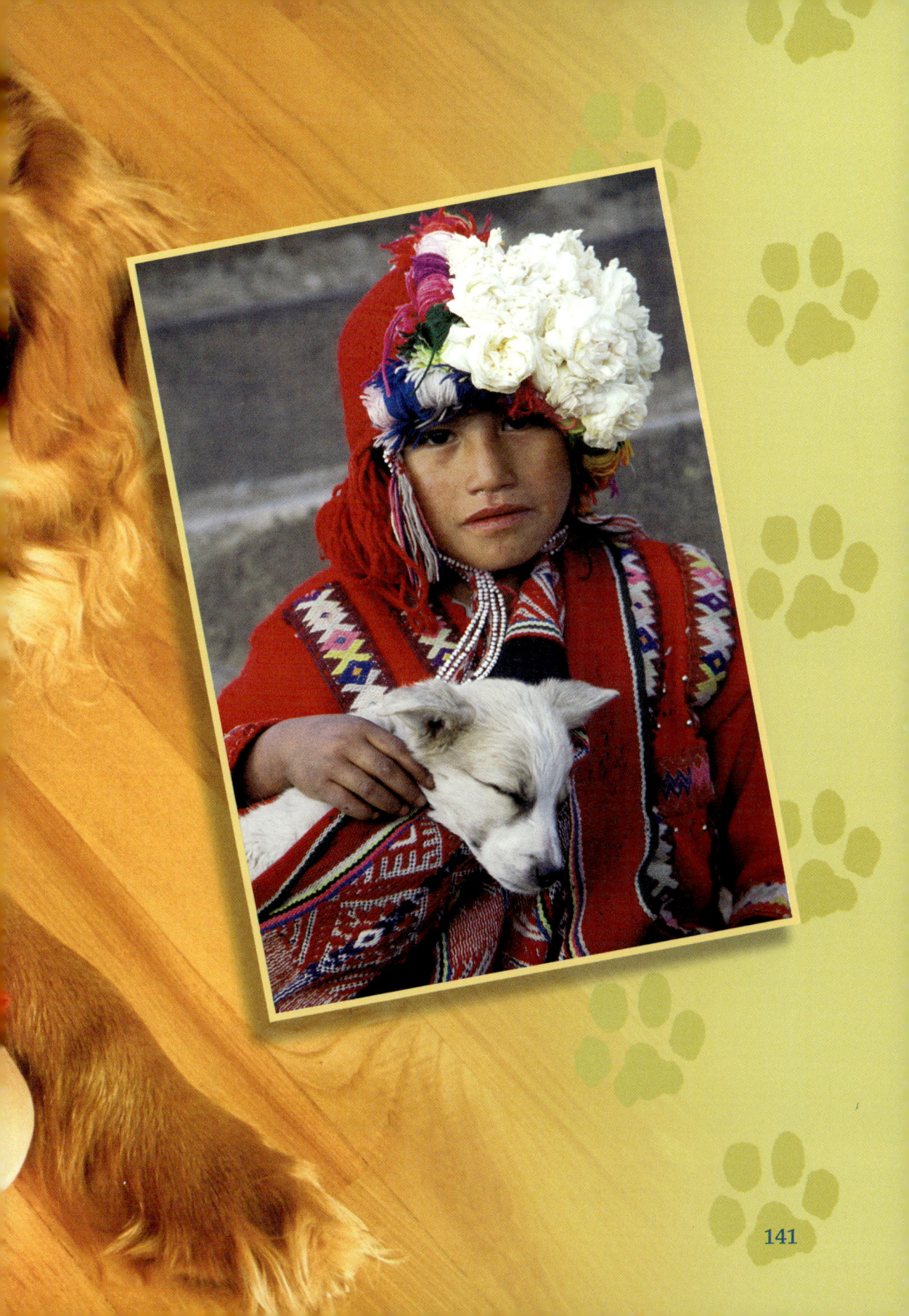

The gathering at Googoorewon

The Aborigines of Australia tell this tale of how dogs came to be. All this happened long, long ago, in the Dreamtime.

Baiame, the Great Spirit, decided to hold a meeting of all the people. So he commanded the tribes to gather in Googoorewon, the place of trees.

Soon the scattered tribes began to arrive. The Baiamul, or Black Swans, arrived shortly before the Du-mer, or Brown Pigeons. Then came the Wahn, or Crows; the Madhi, or Dogs; and many other tribes.

There was great rejoicing as old friends met. Gifts were exchanged. Fires were lighted. The tribes sang and danced. The excitement grew. Why had the Great Spirit called them together? Nobody knew.

At last, Baiame explained. "I have called you together to teach you how to prepare the young men for manhood," he said. "First you must clear a large space for the ceremony."

All but the Madhi, or Dogs, obeyed. The Madhi just stood around watching. At first, no one said anything. Everyone knew the Madhi were lazy. As time passed, the Madhi began to howl with laughter. Still no one paid them much attention. Everyone knew the Madhi were empty-headed.

But when the Madhi began to bark criticisms at the workers, the old medicine men warned them to stop. Instead, the Madhi became louder and sillier. As their bad manners grew worse, Baiame knew that he must punish them.

"You Madhi have not behaved like men," the Great Spirit said. "So, from now on, you will no longer be men. You can sit around and bark and howl all you want!"

One by one, the Madhi dropped to the ground on all fours. Their arms became legs. Their hands and feet became paws. They grew tails. Hair covered their bodies. When they tried to speak, they could only bark and growl, snap and snarl, whimper and whine. These strange new sounds frightened the Madhi. With their tails between their legs, they disappeared into the bush. The Madhi had become the first dogs.

The hound of Hades

Hercules was the greatest of all the many heroes in Greek mythology. He is most famous for the Twelve Labors, or difficult tasks, he performed for his cousin, the king.

As his First Labor, Hercules killed a fierce lion. He then wore the lion's skin as armor. During the next 10 years, Hercules performed 10 even more difficult tasks. Finally, for his last Labor—the most difficult and dangerous of all—the king told Hercules to bring him Cerberus, the fierce, three-headed dog that guarded the gates of Hades, the Kingdom of the Dead.

Cerberus was no ordinary watchdog. His job was to keep people in, not keep people out. So, when Hercules reached the Kingdom of the Dead, Cerberus did not even stir as Hercules entered the gates.

Hercules went directly to the god of the dead, who was called Hades.

"What do you want?" asked Hades.

"I want to take Cerberus to show him to my king," Hercules explained.

"He is yours," replied Hades. "But only if you can take him with your bare hands."

Hercules returned to the gates. But as he approached Cerberus, even the mighty Hercules hesitated. Never had he seen such a monstrous beast. The huge dog had three great heads and a tail like that of a dragon. And around each throat was a ring of hissing snakes.

As Hercules drew nearer, Cerberus leaped for his throat. Hercules caught the dog in midair. He circled his powerful arms around the dog's body and squeezed hard. The snapping jaws reached out to tear him apart, but Hercules was

Dogs in Myth and Legend

protected by the magical lion skin he wore. Then, with a mighty thrust, Hercules raised the choking beast high overhead. And in this way he carried the terrible Cerberus out of the Kingdom of the Dead, all the way to the king's palace.

When he stood before the king, Hercules cried out, "I have completed the Twelfth Labor!" As he said this, he dropped Cerberus to the ground.

Instantly, the dog rushed at the king, who leaped to safety. "Enough!" the king shouted. "I have seen enough! Take that monster back where it belongs!"

Hercules obeyed at once. He had completed the Twelve Labors in 12 years. And from that time on, Cerberus has remained where he belongs—guarding the gates of Hades.

Shiro and the golden coins

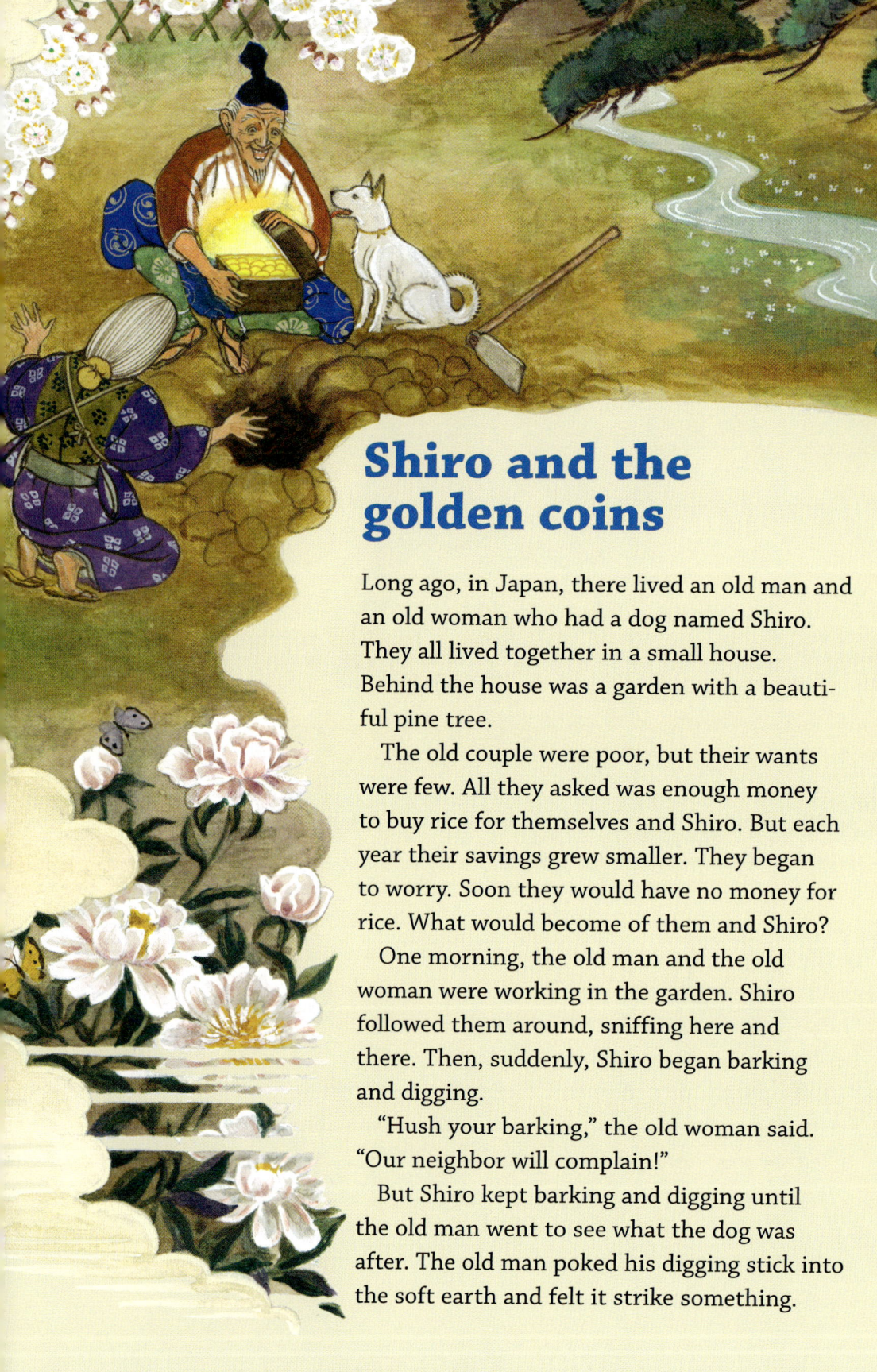

Long ago, in Japan, there lived an old man and an old woman who had a dog named Shiro. They all lived together in a small house. Behind the house was a garden with a beautiful pine tree.

The old couple were poor, but their wants were few. All they asked was enough money to buy rice for themselves and Shiro. But each year their savings grew smaller. They began to worry. Soon they would have no money for rice. What would become of them and Shiro?

One morning, the old man and the old woman were working in the garden. Shiro followed them around, sniffing here and there. Then, suddenly, Shiro began barking and digging.

"Hush your barking," the old woman said. "Our neighbor will complain!"

But Shiro kept barking and digging until the old man went to see what the dog was after. The old man poked his digging stick into the soft earth and felt it strike something.

146   Dogs in Myth and Legend

In a very short time, he had uncovered a small box. When the old couple opened it, they saw to their amazement that it was full of golden coins. Here was enough money to buy rice for the rest of the year!

Their neighbor soon learned of their good fortune and was very jealous. He wanted gold, too. So he dug wherever Shiro sniffed. But he never found a thing. Finally, in a rage, he killed the dog and buried him under the pine tree in the old couple's garden.

The old couple cried when they discovered that Shiro was dead, but there was nothing they could do. Then, one night the ghost of Shiro appeared to them.

"You loved me and cared for me. Now I will take care of you," said Shiro's ghost. "Cut down the pine tree. Then mix some wood chips from the tree into a pot of rice." So saying, the ghost vanished.

The next day the old man chopped down the pine tree. The old woman made a pot of rice. Then they stirred wood chips from the tree into the rice.

"Look," cried the old woman, her eyes filled with wonder. "Each grain of rice is turning into a golden coin. We will have enough money for the rest of our lives."

The old couple smiled sadly as they thought of Shiro. Even in death, their faithful old dog had not forgotten them.

The dog and the fox

Diana, the beautiful Roman goddess of hunting, had many dogs. Her biggest and strongest dog was named Lelaps, which means *storm*. And, like the wind of a storm, Lelaps moved so fast nothing could escape him.

Diana had a good friend, named Procris, who was married to Cephalus, a hunter. Because she wanted to help them, Diana gave them Lelaps. She also gave Cephalus a magical spear that would always hit the mark. With the aid of Lelaps and the spear, Cephalus soon became a mighty hunter.

Now it happened that another goddess became angry with the people and sent a magical fox to pester them. Many hunters tried to catch this fox but could not. The fox was so fast, no hound was able to follow it for long.

Finally, the hunters asked Cephalus for help. "Our hounds are not fast enough to catch this fox sent to pester us," the hunters said. "But Lelaps is as swift as the wind. He can catch the fox. And with your magical spear you can put an end to this fox once and for all."

As soon as Cephalus set Lelaps on the trail of the fox, the dog was off. Lelaps moved with such speed the hunters could not follow him. So they sat on a hillside to watch the chase.

The fox tried every trick. But no matter how fast the fox ran or what tricks it used, Lelaps was always close behind. At last, the fox circled back near the hunters.

It was then that the gods decided to step into the affair. As Cephalus drew back his arm to hurl his spear—the spear that never missed its mark—both fox and dog were turned to stone. The gods had decided that neither dog nor fox should win.

The ribs of the dog

In northern Canada there is a tribe of Indians called the Dogrib. How did the Dogrib tribe get this unusual name?

There is a Dogrib legend that tells of a great quarrel among the people of long ago. After this quarrel, the people went their separate ways.

One Indian built a bark-covered tepee on the edge of a faraway lake. His only companion was his dog, who was expecting a litter. Before long, the puppies were born. They soon grew fat and playful, always eager to follow their master.

The Indian did not want the puppies to follow him into the forest, where they might get lost. So he made each of them a soft, strong collar and leash of buckskin. Whenever he went hunting, he tied the puppies to stakes inside the tepee.

One day as he was returning from the hunt, he heard strange sounds from the tepee. Instead of the barking of puppies, he heard the laughter and chatter of children! But when he entered the tepee he saw only the puppies, who fell over each other in their excitement to greet him.

The Indian was puzzled. Had he only imagined the laughter and voices of children? No, he was sure he had heard children. But where could they have gone?

The next morning, the Indian pretended to go fishing. But instead, he hid in the forest, close by. Soon, the barking of the puppies gave way to the laughter and chatter of children.

Carefully, so as not to make a sound, he crept up to the tepee and silently slipped inside. To his astonishment, he saw a group of happy

Dogs in Myth and Legend

children sitting in a circle about the fire. On the ground behind them lay the skins of the puppies. Before the spell could be broken, he grabbed the skins and threw them into the fire. And so the puppies who had become children remained children.

The children were the beginning of a new tribe. And from that day to this, these people have been known as the Dogrib Indians.

You and Your Dog

153

So you want a puppy

There's a lot more to getting a puppy than just deciding you want one! And there are lots of ways to get one. Someone may give you a **mixed breed.** Perhaps you'll adopt a puppy at an animal shelter. Or you may buy a purebred dog.

If you choose to buy a purebred dog, think about what breed you want. Do you want a dog with long hair or short hair? Do you want a male or female?

Generally speaking, the Sporting Dogs, Hounds, and larger Working Dogs tend to be quieter than most of the Terriers and Toys. A dog with long hair will need more grooming than one with short hair. As a rule, females are less likely to roam than are males. Think about the dog's needs, too. Do you live in an apartment or in a house? Do you have a small yard or lots of land?

Shop around before you pick out a puppy. Find a good kennel that breeds the kind of dog you want. Try to find out a little about the puppy's mother and father. Were they healthy and even-tempered?

It's best to get a puppy when it is from 8 weeks to 3 months old. Look the puppy over carefully. In a healthy pup, the eyes should be clear and bright. How does the pup act? It should be friendly with you and its brothers and sisters. A very shy, unfriendly, or bad-tempered puppy is not likely to change its ways as it gets older.

Plan to take the puppy to a **veterinarian** (animal doctor) right away for a complete checkup. Find out which shots the puppy has had and which ones it needs. And, if you are buying a purebred dog, you'll want to find out about getting proper registration papers and a pedigree.

Finally, unless you plan to breed or to show your dog, have it operated on so it can't have puppies. This should be done whether your dog is a male or a female. And if

You and Your Dog

you do this when your dog is still young—before it is about 6 months old—your dog's basic personality is not likely to change in any way.

A puppy means a big change in your life. It needs lots of loving care. Puppies have "accidents" inside the house while they are being trained. Are you ready to clean up after your puppy? All puppies love to chew on things. Will you watch the puppy and do your best to keep it out of trouble? You'll have a lot of work to do and you'll need lots of patience. But it's worth it—if you really want a puppy!

Puppies, such as these 2-month-old Shi Tzus, are lots of fun and work, but worth it if you really want a puppy.

Where do puppies come from?

Puppies are made when a male and female dog mate. The mother dog is called the **dam.** The father dog is called the **sire.** The puppies grow inside the dam. Each puppy gets food and oxygen through a tube that forms between the puppy and the dam. This tube is called an **umbilical cord.**

About two months after the dam and the sire mate, the puppies are **whelped,** or born. The dam may have from 1 to 10 puppies. Smaller dogs tend to have fewer puppies. Larger dogs have more. The newborn puppies are called a litter.

Each puppy is born inside a see-through bag called a sac. The dam tears open the sac and then bites through the umbilical cord. After this, she licks the puppy until it starts to breathe and is clean and dry.

Sixteen-day-old golden retriever puppies nestle close to their mother to nurse. The pups have not yet opened their eyes.

156 You and Your Dog

A newborn border collie puppy will not be able to see or hear until it is about 2 weeks old.

The puppies snuggle against the warm body of the dam and take milk from her. Their eyes are closed and their ears are sealed. They won't be able to see or hear anything until they're about 2 weeks old. Newborn puppies don't look much like the dogs they will grow up to be. Dalmatian puppies, for example, have no spots. These appear later.

When the puppies are about 4 to 5 weeks old, it is time to start **weaning** them. Weaning simply means getting them used to food other than the dam's milk.

At first, the puppies are fed softened puppy food. During this time they continue to nurse from the dam. By the time the puppies are about 6 weeks old, they will be completely used to eating regular food. They will also be wobbling about, sniffing at all the strange and wonderful smells around them.

During the next few months, the pups will grow quickly, becoming stronger and more active every day.

A beagle puppy has grown old enough to explore the world by itself and has grown enough teeth to chew a ball.

From head to tail

When you want to find out about something, you take a close look. That's because you trust your eyes. But when a dog wants to find out about something, it takes a close smell. That's because a dog trusts its nose.

A dog's nose may be long and pointed, like that of a poodle, or it may be pushed in, flat, and square, like that of a bulldog. Most dogs' noses are black. Some are brown or pink. And some are spotted. But, whatever the color or shape of its nose, a dog's sense of smell is so keen that it recognizes things by smell rather than by sight.

The tip of a dog's nose is usually cold and wet. The moisture comes from a gland inside the nose. The moisture helps the dog detect odors. A cold, moist nose is supposed to be a sign of a healthy dog, but a dog can have a warm, dry nose and still be perfectly healthy.

No two dogs have the same noseprints. A dog's noseprint identifies a dog the same way your fingerprints identify you.

A puppy is blind at birth. Its eyes open about the 10th day. But even when the puppy is fully grown, it will never see as well as you do.

Dogs do not see forms and patterns as well as people do. But their sight is very sensitive to motion. They also do not see very many colors. Dogs see mainly shades of gray and perhaps blue. So most dogs usually depend on their nose and ears more than their eyes.

Dogs' ears come in many shapes and sizes. Some dogs have ears that stand straight up. Some dogs have ears that hang down. And some dogs' ears are partly folded over.

Next to its nose, a dog depends most on its ears. A dog can hear much better than you can. It can also hear very high-pitched sounds that you can't hear.

Some people use special whistles to call their dogs. You could blow with all your might on one of these whistles and

Dogs come in many shapes and sizes. The chihuahua stays small even when it's grown up. The Great Dane is one of the largest of all dogs.

not hear a sound. But a dog would hear it even at a great distance. But don't ever blow this kind of whistle when the dog is close to you. The high-pitched sound can be very painful to the dog.

A puppy is born without teeth but soon gets 28 milk teeth. After about three months, the milk teeth begin to fall out as the permanent teeth grow in. Grown dogs have 42 teeth—10 more than you will have when you grow up. The front teeth—6 in the upper jaw and 6 in the lower jaw—are the incisors. Dogs use these teeth to pick up small objects and to groom themselves. The largest teeth are the 4 canine teeth, or fangs. These are used for holding and tearing. Other teeth, and strong jaw muscles, make it possible for a dog to crush bones.

Dogs tend to gulp their food instead of chewing it as you do. This habit probably comes from their wolf origins. When wolves travel in packs, they have to compete for

A Scottish terrier (left) has two coats—a soft undercoat and a coarse, weather-resistant outercoat; it has a long nose and ears and a tail that stands up straight. By contrast, pugs have short coats, pushed-in noses, ears that fold over, and curled tails.

food. The lucky ones that get to the prey first "wolf" it down fast to get as much of the food for themselves as possible. The strong juices in a dog's stomach help to digest the big lumps of food.

Have you ever wondered why a dog always seems to have its tongue hanging out? It's a dog's way of cooling off. On a hot day, or after a good run, a dog needs extra air. So it sticks out its tongue and pants, or breathes heavily. This gives the dog the extra air it needs to cool off the inside of its body. Also, the water dripping from its tongue is a form of sweat.

A dog's hairy covering is called a coat. This coat is like your clothes. Many dogs have two coats—an undercoat and an outercoat. The soft, dense undercoat keeps the dog warm during cold weather. In warm weather, the dog sheds, or loses, its undercoat. The outercoat protects the dog from rain and snow.

You can tell a lot about a dog's feelings just by watching its tail. When a dog is very pleased or excited, it will wag its tail madly. But when a dog is frightened or in pain, it tucks its tail between its legs.

A dog's tail is sometimes called a rudder. And dogs with long tails do use the tail as a rudder when swimming. Some breeds, though, have naturally short tails. And in other breeds, the tail is **docked,** or cut off short, when the puppies are between 2 and 5 days old.

Why is this done? It may be done to make the dog look more attractive, though many people disagree with this practice today. Long ago, however, docking was often done to avoid paying taxes. Dogs that were used to drive sheep and cattle to market were not taxed. Owners docked the tails of these dogs to show the kind of work they did. Also, in many areas, dogs were taxed according to the length of their tail. The shorter the tail, the less tax the owner had to pay.

An Afghan hound (left) has a very fine, long-haired coat. A whippet's coat is short and smooth and closely hugs its body.

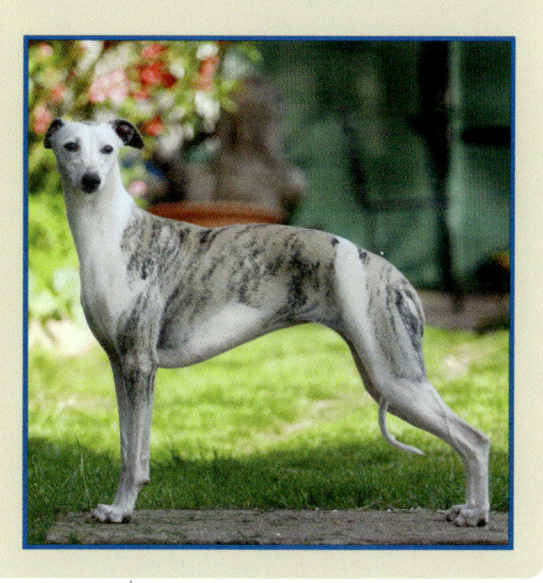

Feeding your dog

A dog always needs water, so keep a bowl of fresh water out all the time. Food is a different story. Your dog will need different amounts and kinds at different ages.

Growing puppies need four meals a day until they're about 3 months old. When you get your pup, ask the veterinarian about the kinds and amount of food it should have. A grown dog needs only one meal a day. How much you feed your dog will depend on its size and the amount of exercise the dog gets. If your dog doesn't eat all its meal in a reasonable time, throw out what's left. And don't worry if your dog skips a meal once in a while. This is perfectly normal.

Never give your dog chicken bones, pork bones, or lamb bones. These bones splinter and the dog could get one caught in its throat. A big beef bone, a rawhide bone, or another kind of chew toy are all better choices.

Make sure your dog's food and water dishes are clean. Germs are just as bad for dogs as they are for you.

Check with your veterinarian about how much—and how often—your dog should eat.

Time for bed

Will your dog live in your house or outdoors in a house of its own? If your dog is going to sleep in the house, fix a place away from drafts, radiators, and heating vents. A small dog does very nicely in a box or basket. A big dog can do very well with an old rug or blanket. Or you can buy a dog bed from a pet store.

Dogs that are kept outside should have a safe, fenced-in area and a good doghouse. The floor of the doghouse should be off the ground to keep out the damp. The roof should be hinged to make the house easier to clean. A carpet or canvas flap over the opening will help keep out the wind and rain. For bedding, use cedar shavings, shredded newspapers, or old blankets.

Whether you keep your dog inside or outside, be sure to keep the bedding fresh and clean.

A beagle snuggles into its dog bed. A dog bed doesn't have to be store-bought. Just be sure it is soft, clean, and big enough for your dog.

Bathing and grooming

Lucky dog! It doesn't need a bath every day. In fact, too many baths can remove natural oils and make a dog's coat dry and harsh. So don't give your dog a bath unless it becomes really dirty or smelly.

Regular grooming is the best way to keep a dog clean and looking good. Dogs with short hair should be brushed. Dogs with long hair should be carefully combed and then brushed.

When you have to give your dog a bath, a laundry sink, large plastic basin, or bathtub is the best place to do it. To keep the dog from sliding about, put a bath mat or heavy towel in the tub. Stand the dog in the tub and plug its ears with cotton to protect them from soapy water.

Run in warm water up to about the middle of the dog's legs. Wet the dog and then work up a good lather with mild soap, a dog soap, or a dog shampoo. Work from the head toward the tail. Be sure to avoid getting soap in its eyes. When finished, rinse the dog well.

Wrap the dog in a big towel before it has a chance to shake itself. Rub the dog briskly until it is as dry as possible. Keep the dog out of drafts until it is completely dry. Then finish the job with a good combing and brushing.

Dogs with long hair, such as this cocker spaniel, should have their hair combed before being brushed.

You and Your Dog

Housebreaking your puppy

Housebreaking—teaching your new puppy not to go to the bathroom in the house—is the first step in training. Until the pup is housebroken, keep it in an area with a linoleum or tile floor. Or, put the pup in a crate or cage that's large enough for the puppy to move around. Fix up a box for the dog to sleep in and put down newspapers.

Take the pup for a walk the first thing in the morning and the last thing at night. Don't leave water out for it at night. Take it out about an hour after each feeding. If possible, take the pup out even if it just looks as if it has to go. And praise your puppy when it does go outside!

When accidents happen, don't hit your dog. Just scold it with your voice. Say, "No! Bad dog!" If you can, take it out right away. And praise it whether it goes or not.

You may have to leave the pup alone for hours at a time. If so, it's a good idea to paper-train the dog. Confine the puppy—or put it in a crate or cage—and put down papers as before. After a few days, leave part of the floor or crate area bare. If the pup goes on the bare floor, scold it and put it on the papers. Praise the dog when it uses the papers. The puppy will soon learn to go on the papers if it can't get outside. In time, it will be able to control itself between walks and you can take up the papers.

Housebreaking takes time and patience. Don't expect quick results. And don't give your pup the run of the house until it is housebroken. Then, you can teach it to leave things alone and to stay off the furniture.

You can paper-train your puppy if you know you won't be able to take it out often enough.

Training your dog

A well-trained dog is a joy to see and a joy to own. When people enjoy meeting or being with your dog, you will feel a tremendous sense of pride.

Serious training should begin when your dog is about 6 months old. By that time, your dog should be used to a collar and leash and able to understand the meaning of "No!" And your dog will be old enough to remember the things it is taught.

Before you begin the training, there are a few things you should know. When your dog doesn't do what you want, correct it instantly. Make sure it obeys *every* command you give. Correction may be a harsh "No!" or simply pushing it into the position you want.

Never strike your dog. Don't even threaten it with your hand. Your dog will learn to see every upraised hand as a threat. And don't shout. Praise your dog in a warm, friendly voice. Scold it in a harsh voice.

When you scold your dog is very important. Never scold it after you have called it to you or it has come to you itself. Your dog will think it's being scolded for coming, not for what it did before that.

If your dog is some distance away when it does something wrong, just get it under control and start the lesson again.

A well-trained dog should know the six basic commands: heel, sit, stay, stand-stay, down, and come. The commands should be taught in that order. The dog must learn to obey instantly, after only one command.

Try to have two short training periods each day. Fifteen to 30 minutes is plenty of time. Any more and the dog may get restless. Find a quiet place, inside or outside, where the two of you can be alone. Keep the dog on the leash at all times so that it is under your control. Don't work your dog off the leash until it has mastered all six commands.

For training purposes, you'll want a chain or leather choke collar. This kind of collar tightens around the dog's throat when you give the leash a jerk or the dog tries to pull away. Never use constant pressure. A quick jerk and release will do the trick. Training is not a test of strength; it is a test of will.

Make sure the dog has mastered a particular command before you try to teach it another one. If it has trouble, go back to the last command so that you can praise your dog. Especially at first, a dog cookie or similar treat is a good form of praise. Always end a lesson with praise.

As training goes on, things will get easier. The dog will learn that a command means that it is to do something. The dog just has to learn what it is supposed to do.

Dog Tracks

Does your puppy have a bellybutton?

It sure does! You can't see it very easily because it's very small and covered with hair. But because puppies grow inside their mothers the same way human babies do, puppies have an umbilical cord just like human babies. After a puppy is born, its mother bites off the umbilical cord, leaving a scar—a bellybutton. Because a puppy's umbilical cord is small, so is its bellybutton. You might be able to see it when your puppy is lying on its back. Look very closely in the middle of its tummy. The bellybutton is a small slit that may have a swirl of fur around it.

Heel: On this command, your dog should walk at your left side, about even with your left knee.

Snap on the leash. Take the free end in your right hand. With your left hand, hold the leash near the collar so that the dog has to walk close to you.

As you move forward, say the dog's name, then, "Heel!" On the word "Heel!" give the leash a quick, gentle, jerk. If the dog starts to move ahead or lag behind, give the leash a jerk and say "Heel!" When the dog is back in position, praise it. Never pull, or allow the dog to pull, on the leash. Just use a quick jerk and then release the pressure.

With practice, your dog will stay by your left knee as you walk, trot, make turns, and go in circles. In time, your dog will heel on or off the leash. When it has mastered the heel, go on to the sit.

Sit: Teach the sit while your dog is heeling. It should learn to sit, without command, the moment you stop.

Walk with your dog at heel. With your right hand, grasp the leash just below your left hand. Take your left hand off the leash. Then stop and give the command, "Sit!" At the same time, pull up on the leash with your right hand and push down on the dog's hindquarters with your left hand.

Hold the dog in this position and praise it. Then give the command to heel and start walking. After a few steps, repeat the sit. As the dog begins to get the idea, you can stop giving the command to sit. Finally, you can stop guiding it with your hand and the leash.

When your dog will sit without command or help the moment you stop walking, you can begin teaching it to sit on command from any position. Stand the dog in front of you and give the command to sit. As before, guide the dog with your left hand and the leash. When it has mastered the sit at heel or from any other position, you can introduce the command to stay.

You and Your Dog

Stay: The command to stay should be taught while your dog is sitting. In the stay, your dog must sit without moving until you give it another command.

Snap on the leash and command the dog to sit. Then, hold your hand up in front of its nose and in a firm voice say, "Stay!" Repeat the command. If necessary, use your hands to hold the dog in position.

The first few times, don't make the dog stay more than about ten seconds. Repeat the command to stay as often as necessary. Then release the dog with an "Okay!" And be sure to praise it for a job well done.

In the following lessons, you can increase the time of the stay until the dog will hold the sit for at least three minutes. When your dog is able to do this, you are ready to go on to the stand-stay.

Stand-Stay: This command teaches your dog to stand in place. It can be a big help when you groom your pet.

Start by teaching this command while your dog is heeling. As you slow down, say, "Stand!" and pull back on the leash. At the same time, put your left hand in front of the upper part of the dog's right hind leg. This will keep it from sitting, which it will start to do. If it does sit, don't scold your dog. It's only doing what it has already learned. Just start again. When you have the dog standing, continue to say, "Stand!" Then tell it, "Stay!"

Practice the heel and sit and the heel and stand. Your dog will learn to listen for a command and, if there is no command, to sit.

You can now teach the stand-stay. With the dog in the stand position, hold your hand in front of its nose and say, "Stay!" Then, holding the leash, take a step away. If the dog starts to move, say, "No, stay!" Slowly increase the time until it can hold the stand-stay for one minute as you move around it.

When the dog has learned this lesson, you can begin the down lesson.

Traveling with your dog

What should you do with your dog when you go on vacation? If you don't take the dog with you, you may put it in a boarding kennel or find a dog sitter or friend to take care of it. But what if you want to take your dog with you?

First, check with the places in which you plan to stay. Dogs may not be welcome. If you're going by car, get a folding wire cage or seat harness for the dog. It will keep the dog from moving around in the car and distracting the driver and from jumping out when a door is opened. And never leave your dog in the car with the windows closed, even for a few minutes. In hot weather, a dog can die very quickly in a closed car.

When making a stop, give the dog water and take it for a walk. Put the leash on before you open the door—and keep it on. If your dog gets loose, it might get lost or hurt. Just in case, put a special identification tag on your dog's collar that contains a telephone number at which you can be reached. Your home address and phone number won't help if you are away from home.

If you're traveling by train or plane, you will have to make special arrangements for shipping the dog. Dogs must usually travel in special crates, in the baggage section. So check well in advance with the railroad or the airline to find out what you have to do.

This dog is ready for a trip! By placing your dog in a travel crate, you can be sure that it will not move around in the car and distract the driver or jump out suddenly when a door is opened.

You and Your Dog

Lost dog

A lost dog is sad to see. It runs around searching for familiar places. It sniffs at everyone, hoping to find its owner. It darts across busy streets, in danger of being hurt. The dog becomes tired, frightened, and thirsty.

If the dog is lucky enough to have a smart, responsible owner, it will be wearing tags. One tag shows that the dog has had its yearly rabies shot. Another tag is the dog's license. And still another tag shows the owner's name, address, and phone number. Anyone who finds the dog can contact the owner, and soon the dog will be home!

Be sure that your dog always wears a tag with your name, address, and phone number. That way, if the dog becomes lost, whoever finds it can contact you.

Not all stray dogs are so lucky. Many strays are killed by cars. Others, without tags, are taken to a pound. A pound is a place where stray animals are kept for a short time. If nobody claims the animal, it may be sold, turned over to an animal shelter, or put to death.

Don't let this happen to your dog. Be sure that your dog does not run loose. Walk your dog on a leash. At home, keep your dog in a fenced-in dog run or on a long chain attached to a stake or overhead wire. See that your dog always wears its collar and tags. Or, you might have your vet insert a microchip under your dog's skin. Such chips contain an identification code that can be read by a special device. Either way, anyone who finds your dog will be able to find you. If your dog is ever missing, call your local police department, the dog shelters in your area, and the dog pound.

Dogs to Know

175

Breeds of dogs

What kind of dog do you like best? If you like purebred dogs, there are many different kinds.

There are 162 breeds shown and described here and on the following pages. These include the 157 breeds registered by the American Kennel Club (AKC) as well as the 5 breeds the AKC now admits to the Miscellaneous Class.

Dog Groups

Sporting Group
Hound Group
Working Group
Herding Group
Terrier Group
Toy Group
Nonsporting Group
Miscellaneous Class

The dogs are drawn approximately to scale and are shown as they appear when full-grown. This way, you can see how big—or how small—one dog is compared with another.

The short paragraph next to each picture tells you some of the things you might want to know about the breed. At the end of the paragraph you will find the group to which the AKC assigns the breed.

Affenpinscher (*AH fuhn pihn shuhr*) is a small, lively bundle of energy. It has a stiff, wiry, shaggy coat. Its German name means *monkey terrier*. The affenpinscher is a playful pet and a fine house dog. [Toy Group]

Afghan hound (*AF guhn*) gets its name from the country of Afghanistan, where it was once a royal hunting dog. This large, swift, high-leaping hound hunts by sight. Although proud-looking, the Afghan loves to play. Its long, silky coat needs lots of care. [Hound Group]

Airedale terrier is the largest dog in the Terrier Group. This wiry-coated dog is named for the Aire Valley in northern England. Absolutely fearless, the Airedale is also loving and gentle. [Terrier Group]

Dogs to Know

Akita *(ah KEE tah)* is a strong dog with a short, rough coat and a curly tail. The breed comes from Japan, where it is still revered. Bred as a hunter, the Akita is now used as a police and guard dog. It is also a faithful family dog. [Working Group]

Alaskan malamute *(MAH luh myoot)* is a native Alaskan dog. It is named for the Inuit people called Malamutes, who bred it as a sled dog. A strong, rugged animal, the malamute has a thick, heavy coat and enjoys the coldest weather. This friendly, lovable dog makes an excellent pet. [Working Group]

American Eskimo dog has a white-to-cream coat with especially thick fur around the neck, chest, and hind legs. Once called the American spitz, it was popular at circuses because it can be trained to do tricks. Even though it is a friendly dog, it makes a good watchdog because it is smart and alert. [Nonsporting Group]

American foxhound was bred to hunt foxes and is not often kept as a pet. Strong and fast, it hunts by scent and can stay on the trail for hours. When a foxhound bays as it follows the scent, its deep voice can be heard over great distances. These dogs are trained to hunt alone or in packs. *See also* English foxhound. [Hound Group]

American Staffordshire terrier was first bred in the United States as a heavier variety of the Staffordshire bull terrier of England. It has a short, stiff coat and makes a good watchdog. *See also* Staffordshire bull terrier. [Terrier Group]

American water spaniel is a fine, all-around hunting dog. Its thick, curly coat protects it from cold water and thorny bushes. Eager to please, it both flushes and retrieves. *See also* Irish water spaniel. [Sporting Group]

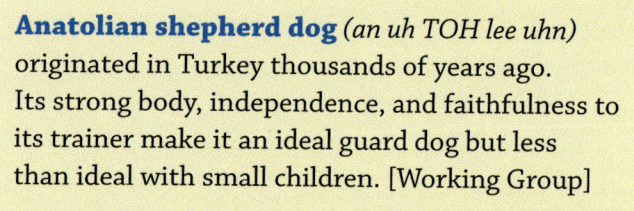

Anatolian shepherd dog *(an uh TOH lee uhn)* originated in Turkey thousands of years ago. Its strong body, independence, and faithfulness to its trainer make it an ideal guard dog but less than ideal with small children. [Working Group]

Australian cattle dog was bred in Australia. Now popular there as a show dog, it is still widely used to herd cattle. A fast, smart worker, it is also a fine pet and very good with children. [Herding Group]

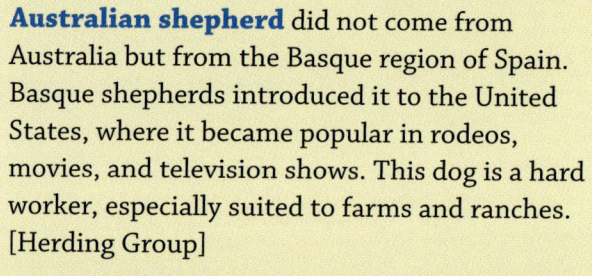

Australian shepherd did not come from Australia but from the Basque region of Spain. Basque shepherds introduced it to the United States, where it became popular in rodeos, movies, and television shows. This dog is a hard worker, especially suited to farms and ranches. [Herding Group]

Australian terrier was bred to hunt rodents and other small animals but is now mostly a pet. It has a harsh, straight coat and a soft-haired topknot. An ideal house dog, it is very patient with children. [Terrier Group]

Basenji *(buh SEHN jee)* is a hunting dog that comes from central Africa. This dog does not bark but makes a whining sound when happy. It has a short, silky coat. The basenji is very intelligent and loves to play. [Hound Group]

Basset hound is a short-legged, short-haired hunting dog with a long, heavy body and a sad-looking face. Its name comes from the French word *bas,* meaning "low." The friendly basset is a good family dog. [Hound Group]

Beagle is a small hunting dog with a smooth coat. A favorite for hunting rabbits, this dog will work alone or in a pack. The gentle, affectionate beagle is a good dog for the country or the city. [Hound Group]

Dogs to Know

Bearded collie is named for the hairs around its muzzle. Unlike other collies, the bearded collie has a harsh, shaggy coat and a blunt head. The bearded collie is a fine sheepdog and a good family pet. [Herding Group]

Beauceron *(BOH sur ohn)* is a very large sheepdog named after Beauce, the region in France where it originated and is still popular. In addition to being useful for herding sheep and cattle, it excels in search-and-rescue work. The Beauceron is a serious dog that trains well and makes a faithful companion. [Herding Group]

Bedlington terrier is a dog that looks like a lamb. Its soft, fleecy coat should be kept trimmed. The breed is named for Bedlington, England, where it was first bred. [Terrier Group]

Belgian Malinois *(mal uh NWAH)* is named after the town in Belgium where it was first bred. It has a short, fawn-colored coat and is often mistaken for the kind of dog that is called a German shepherd. Very intelligent and alert, the Malinois is a good watchdog. [Herding Group]

Belgian sheepdog is closely related to the Malinois but its coat is long and black. At one time, this dog, the Malinois, and a dog called the Tervuren were all called Belgian sheepdogs. Now, only the black-haired dog is known by this name. It is often used for police work. [Herding Group]

Belgian Tervuren *(TUR vurn)* is closely related to the Malinois and the Belgian sheepdog. It has a long coat of fawn- or mahogany-colored, black-tipped hair. Named for the town of Tervuren, Belgium, the Tervuren was bred as a sheepdog. Like most sheepdogs, it is alert, intelligent, and loyal. [Herding Group]

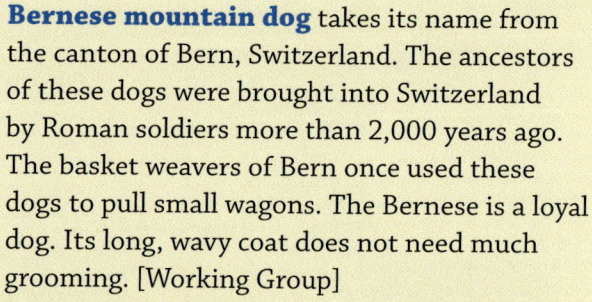

Bernese mountain dog takes its name from the canton of Bern, Switzerland. The ancestors of these dogs were brought into Switzerland by Roman soldiers more than 2,000 years ago. The basket weavers of Bern once used these dogs to pull small wagons. The Bernese is a loyal dog. Its long, wavy coat does not need much grooming. [Working Group]

Bichon frise (BEE shahn free ZAY) is a very lively little dog whose French name means *curly lap dog*. And the curly-haired bichon has been a lap dog for hundreds of years. Sailors of long ago traded these sturdy, smart dogs in ports all around the world. The bichon's thick, loose curls need grooming. [Nonsporting Group]

Black and tan coonhound is the only kind of coonhound recognized by the AKC as purebred. This dog hunts by scent. Its specialty is the raccoon, but it is also used to hunt larger animals. It has a short, thick coat that is black and tan. [Hound Group]

Black Russian terrier became a breed in the Soviet Union (now Russia) during the 1950's, when the Communist government needed a dog that would work in prisons and on military bases. As a result, the Russian terrier is a powerful and courageous dog that is trained mainly for protecting its owner. [Working Group]

Bloodhound is a dog famous for its ability to follow a scent. Often used to find lost people, this gentle dog will not attack a person. A loving dog, it makes an excellent pet. Its name is short for *blooded hound*. *Blooded* is a term used for an animal that comes from good stock. [Hound Group]

180   Dogs to Know

Border collie is a dog that has helped to herd sheep in all parts of the world. Also known as the farm collie or working collie, it is one of the finest of all sheepdogs. The border collie is an alert watchdog, makes a fine pet, and is good with children. [Herding Group]

Border terrier is an old English breed that comes from the border country of northern England. A small hunting dog, it is now bred mainly as a family pet. [Terrier Group]

Borzoi (BAWR zoy) is a tall, lean hunting dog with a long, silky coat. This dog used to be called a Russian wolfhound. The name *borzoi* is the Russian word for *swift*. [Hound Group]

Boston terrier was first bred in Boston about 100 years ago. It is part English bulldog and part terrier. Gentle, smart, and courageous, the Boston likes people and is a favorite family pet. [Nonsporting Group]

Bouvier des Flandres (boo VYAY day FLAHN druh) has a rough, wiry coat. Its name means *cowherd of Flanders*. It is a good herder and watchdog. [Herding Group]

Boxer is a strong, stocky dog with a short, shiny coat. Playful and patient with children, it makes a good family pet. It is also often used for police work. No one is sure how the boxer got its name, but it may be from the way it uses its front paws in a fight. [Working Group]

Briard (bree AHRD) comes from France and is named for its home, the district of Brie. This dog has a heavy, shaggy coat and likes to be outdoors. It is often used on farms and ranches to help herd cattle and sheep. Fearless and faithful, the briard is an excellent watchdog. [Herding Group]

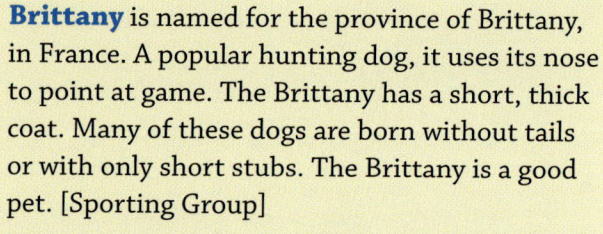

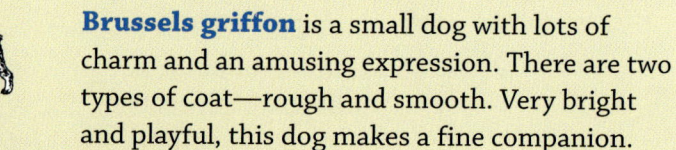

Brittany is named for the province of Brittany, in France. A popular hunting dog, it uses its nose to point at game. The Brittany has a short, thick coat. Many of these dogs are born without tails or with only short stubs. The Brittany is a good pet. [Sporting Group]

Brussels griffon is a small dog with lots of charm and an amusing expression. There are two types of coat—rough and smooth. Very bright and playful, this dog makes a fine companion. [Toy Group]

Bulldog is the national dog of Great Britain. This dog is short and heavy, with a smooth coat. In spite of its looks, the bulldog is very gentle and loves children. [Nonsporting Group]

Bullmastiff is a cross between the mastiff and the bulldog. It is a big, strong dog with a short, heavy coat. Fearless, alert, and obedient, the bullmastiff makes a good family watchdog. [Working Group]

Bull terrier comes in two varieties—white and colored. This dog was bred in England as a fighting dog. Good-natured, the bull terrier makes a fine companion. [Terrier Group]

Cairn terrier is a small dog with a hard, shaggy coat. It got its name from its ability to go after small animals in heaps of stones called cairns. Easy to care for, the cairn terrier is at home anywhere. [Terrier Group]

Canaan dog is the national dog of Israel. It is an intelligent dog that has been used as a sentry, a land-mine locator, and a guide dog for people who are visually impaired. [Herding Group]

Cardigan Welsh corgi (KAWR gee) has a dense, medium-length coat and a tail like a fox. The name corgi means *dwarf dog*. A herd dog, the corgi is also a good house dog. *See also* Pembroke Welsh corgi. [Herding Group]

Dogs to Know

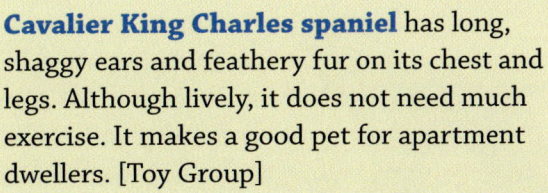

Cavalier King Charles spaniel has long, shaggy ears and feathery fur on its chest and legs. Although lively, it does not need much exercise. It makes a good pet for apartment dwellers. [Toy Group]

Chesapeake Bay retriever is a hunting dog with a short, thick coat. This dog can work in cold, rough water for a long time. Many people think it is the best of all the retrievers. The Chesapeake was named for the area in the United States where it was first bred. [Sporting Group]

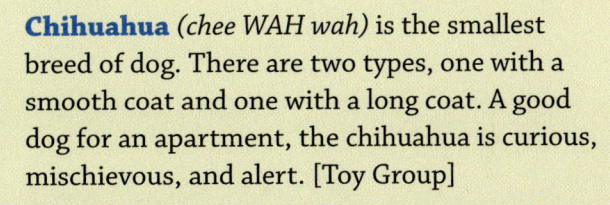

Chihuahua *(chee WAH wah)* is the smallest breed of dog. There are two types, one with a smooth coat and one with a long coat. A good dog for an apartment, the chihuahua is curious, mischievous, and alert. [Toy Group]

Chinese crested dog has no coat. Its skin is bare except for a tuft of hair on its forehead and some hair on its tail. [Toy Group]

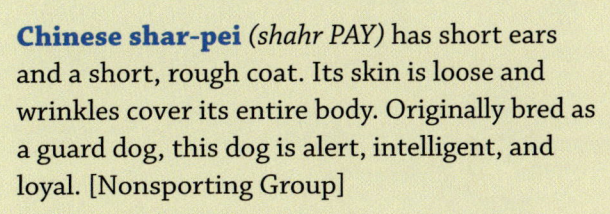

Chinese shar-pei *(shahr PAY)* has short ears and a short, rough coat. Its skin is loose and wrinkles cover its entire body. Originally bred as a guard dog, this dog is alert, intelligent, and loyal. [Nonsporting Group]

Chow chow, usually called just chow, comes from China. It is the only breed of dog that has a blue-black tongue. A medium-sized dog, the chow chow is strong, active, and intelligent. [Nonsporting Group]

Clumber spaniel gets its name from an English country estate, Clumber Park. The largest and heaviest of the land spaniels, the Clumber has a silky white coat with orange- or lemon-colored markings. [Sporting Group]

Cocker spaniel has a soft, thick coat. The smallest of the Sporting Dogs, it is also known as the American cocker. Gentle and playful, the cocker is a very popular dog, loves children, and is more likely to be kept as a pet than used for hunting. [Sporting Group]

Collie was first bred in Scotland to herd sheep. There are two types, the familiar rough collie and the seldom-seen smooth collie. The dogs are alike except for their coats. *See also* Bearded collie; Border collie. [Herding Group]

Coonhound, *see* Black and tan coonhound.

Corgi, *see* Cardigan Welsh corgi; Pembroke Welsh corgi.

Curly-coated retriever is named for its tight, curly coat, which usually requires a fair amount of grooming. This dog is active and loves to swim. Faithful and intelligent, it is easily trained, a good hunting dog, and a wonderful companion. [Sporting Group]

Dachshund *(DAHKS hund)* comes from Germany. Its name means *badger hound*. There are three varieties—smooth, longhaired, and wirehaired. All three kinds come in two sizes—standard and miniature. Lively and fun-loving, the dachshund is a popular pet. [Hound Group]

Dalmatian *(dal MAY shun)* is named for the district of Dalmatia in Croatia. Hardy and clean, the Dalmatian is a good family pet and a fine watchdog. [Nonsporting Group]

Dandie Dinmont terrier is named for a farmer in a book by Scottish author Sir Walter Scott. This playful dog has a shaggy coat and hind legs that are longer than its front legs. [Terrier Group]

Doberman pinscher (*DOH buhr muhn PIHN shuhr*) is a short-haired dog that was bred in Germany for police work. The Doberman is fearless, alert, and obedient. *See also* German pinscher; Miniature pinscher [Working Group]

Dogue de Bordeaux (*dawg dee bohr DOH*) is a powerful, muscular dog that arose in France. It was originally used to hunt and to herd and guard cattle. A calm, non aggressive dog, it is very devoted to its master. [Miscellaneous Class]

English cocker spaniel is bigger than its American cousin. Intelligent and willing, the English cocker is a good hunter and cheerful family dog. [Sporting Group]

English foxhound is one of the oldest breeds of hound. Trained to hunt in packs, these dogs are sturdy, with straight legs and short, dense coats. Because most foxhounds would rather hunt than be around people, very few of these dogs are kept as pets. *See also* American foxhound. [Hound Group]

English setter is thought by many people to be one of the most beautiful of all dogs. It has a medium-length, flat coat and a straight, well-feathered tail. It is a born hunter and is better suited to the country than the city. Graceful and gentle, the English setter is a good family dog. [Sporting Group]

English springer spaniel got its name from the way it hunts—it makes the game "spring" from its hiding place. Friendly and smart, the English springer is a popular hunting dog that works well on land and in water. It is a good retriever. [Sporting Group]

English toy spaniel has a long, silky coat. There are two varieties—solid color and broken color. These little dogs have long been a favorite of English royalty. [Toy Group]

Field spaniel is a hunting dog with a flat, shiny coat, usually black. Intelligent and obedient, this hard-working spaniel retrieves well on land or in water. [Sporting Group]

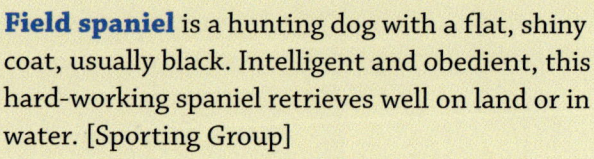

Finnish spitz *(spits)* was originally bred in Finland and Lapland as a hunting and watchdog. Resembling a fox, this dog has a long, reddish-brown coat. [Nonsporting Group]

Flat-coated retriever has a dense, sleek coat, usually black or liver-colored. A good hunter and companion, this dog is a strong swimmer and loves water. [Sporting Group]

Foxhound, *see* American foxhound; English foxhound.

Fox terrier, *see* Smooth fox terrier; Toy fox terrier; Wire fox terrier.

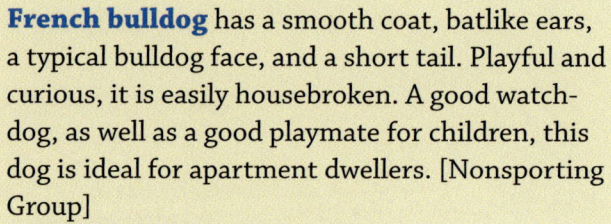

French bulldog has a smooth coat, batlike ears, a typical bulldog face, and a short tail. Playful and curious, it is easily housebroken. A good watchdog, as well as a good playmate for children, this dog is ideal for apartment dwellers. [Nonsporting Group]

German pinscher developed in Germany in the late 1800's and became the source for two related breeds, the Doberman pinscher and the miniature pinscher. It has a short coat and square, muscular body. This pinscher makes an excellent watchdog and companion. *See also* Doberman pinscher; Miniature pinscher. [Working Group]

German shepherd dog was first bred in Germany as a herd dog. Later, it was used as a war dog. Today, this intelligent dog is used for police work and as a guard dog, a guide dog for the visually impaired, and a rescue dog. A loyal family dog, the German shepherd is good with children. [Herding Group]

German shorthaired pointer is a hunting dog with a short, hard coat. Although it works more slowly than setters or other pointers, the shorthair is a good, all-around hunting dog that can hunt and retrieve almost any kind of game in the field or water. [Sporting Group]

German wirehaired pointer has a dense, soft undercoat and a rough, wiry outercoat that gives it good protection in rough brush or cold water. This all-purpose hunter, developed in Germany, works well on land or in water and is a good retriever. [Sporting Group]

Giant schnauzer *(SHNOW zuhr)* was developed in Germany to help drive cattle to market. Its name means *snout* or *muzzle*. This dog has a shaggy muzzle and shaggy eyebrows. It is a loyal family dog. *See also* Miniature schnauzer; Standard schnauzer. [Working Group]

Glen of Imaal terrier gets its name from the countryside of the Imaal *(EE mahl)* valley in Ireland. It was bred to help with chores around the house. This long, squat dog is gentle and loves to run. [Terrier Group]

Golden retriever has a thick, flat or wavy double coat and lots of feathering. First bred in Scotland, the self-confident golden is eager to please and easy to train. A fine field or water dog, the golden is also an excellent family dog. [Sporting Group]

Gordon setter was named after a Scottish nobleman. Its long, soft coat may be flat or slightly waved. Like other setters, it marks game by pointing with its nose. A fine pet, it is gentle with children. [Sporting Group]

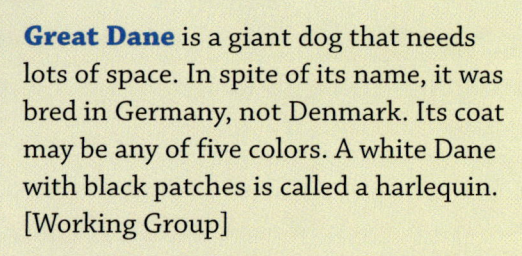

Great Dane is a giant dog that needs lots of space. In spite of its name, it was bred in Germany, not Denmark. Its coat may be any of five colors. A white Dane with black patches is called a harlequin. [Working Group]

Great Pyrenees (PIHR uh neez) is a large dog with a long, flat, heavy coat. It was named for the mountains between France and Spain, where it was used to herd sheep. The Pyrenees is a good dog around children. [Working Group]

Greater Swiss mountain dog is a large, powerful dog. It is the largest of the Swiss mountain dogs. It has a short, black and tan coat with white markings. It was used to pull dairy carts in Switzerland. [Working Group]

Greyhound was known in Egypt more than 3,000 years ago. It hunts by sight and is the fastest of all dogs. The greyhound is best known as a racing dog. [Hound Group]

Griffon, see Brussels griffon; Petit basset griffon vendéen; Wirehaired pointing griffon.

Harrier (HAR ee uhr) has a short, flat coat and looks like a small English foxhound. It hunts by scent and was bred to chase hares, which are large relatives of the rabbit. Harriers usually hunt in packs. [Hound Group]

Havanese came first from an island in the Mediterranean Sea. But its name refers to the city of Havana in Cuba, where it became especially popular. This clever breed, related to the bichon frise, loves attention and playing with children; however, it can be mischievous. [Toy Group]

Husky, see Siberian husky.

Ibizan hound (ee BEE sahn) comes from the island of Ibiza in the Mediterranean Sea. Its coat is either short and silky or long, thick, and wiry. This dog hunts by scent, points, and retrieves. [Hound Group]

Irish red and white setter originated in Ireland, just as the Irish setter did. For many years, the red and white was the lesser known of the two breeds, though it probably developed before the red Irish setter did. A friendly, athletic dog, the red and white setter is mainly used for hunting. [Miscellaneous Class]

Irish setter has a silky, dark-red coat. Bred in Ireland, this hunting dog is spirited, gentle, and lovable. Its coat is a rich mahogany color. Although a good gundog, this setter is more popular as a pet. [Sporting Group]

Irish terrier, one of the oldest of all the terrier breeds, does not look like any other terrier. It has a hard, wiry, medium-length coat. Fearless and bold, the Irish terrier was used to carry messages on battlefields. This dog is a fine companion for a child. [Terrier Group]

Irish water spaniel has a curly coat, a topknot on its head, and a thin, so-called "rat tail." This hunting dog is a strong swimmer, works best in water, and is particularly good at retrieving ducks and other water birds. *See also* American water spaniel. [Sporting Group]

Irish wolfhound, the tallest of all dogs, has a rough, wiry coat. Though bred to hunt wolves, this hound is one of the gentlest of all breeds. It is dignified and quiet but needs plenty of room. [Hound Group]

Italian greyhound looks like a miniature greyhound. This dog has been a popular pet since Roman times. It has large, expressive eyes and a short, sleek coat. [Toy Group]

Japanese chin has a silky, feathery coat. There are several types and colors, but most are black and white. This dog's original home was China. [Toy Group]

Keeshond *(KAYS hahnd),* the national dog of the Netherlands, is named after a famous Dutch patriot. This dog has a thick, straight coat and is a fine companion. [Nonsporting Group]

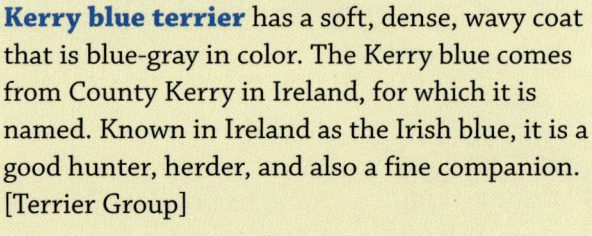

Kerry blue terrier has a soft, dense, wavy coat that is blue-gray in color. The Kerry blue comes from County Kerry in Ireland, for which it is named. Known in Ireland as the Irish blue, it is a good hunter, herder, and also a fine companion. [Terrier Group]

Komondor *(KOH mahn dawr)* is a shepherd dog from Hungary. Its thick coat makes it look as if it is covered with long cords. One of the oldest breeds in Europe, the komondor is an excellent guard dog but may be a difficult pet to handle. [Working Group]

Kuvasz *(KOO vahz)* is a large, strong dog with a pure white coat. Its ancestors came from Tibet, but the breed was developed in Hungary. Its name comes from a Turkish word that means *armed guard of the nobility*. [Working Group]

Labrador retriever, perhaps the most popular retriever, is also a fine family dog. In spite of its name, it comes from Newfoundland, not Labrador. Its coat may be black, yellow, or chocolate in color. [Sporting Group]

Lakeland terrier was first bred in the Lake District of northern England, where it was used to hunt foxes and otters. Bold but friendly, the small, sturdy Lakeland is a good family dog. [Terrier Group]

Lhasa apso (LAH suh AP soh) has a long, heavy coat that needs a lot of grooming. Originally from Lhasa, the capital of Tibet, it is known as the "lion dog." In Tibet, this dog is an indoor watchdog. [Nonsporting Group]

Löwchen (LOH chuhn) originated more than 500 years ago in Europe, where breeders gave it a sturdy body and a mane like that of a lion. This proud-looking dog is smart, easy to train, and makes an ideal pet. [Nonsporting Group]

Malamute, see Alaskan malamute.

Maltese was probably developed on the island of Malta more than 2,000 years ago. This spirited little animal may have been the first lap dog. It has a long, silky white coat that needs care. [Toy Group]

Manchester terrier is a breed that comes in two varieties, toy and standard. Named for Manchester, England, these dogs are very clean house dogs. [Terrier Group and Toy Group]

Mastiff, or **Old English mastiff,** is a giant dog with a short coat. Although bred long ago as a fighting dog, the mastiff is good-natured. It makes a fine family dog for people who like really big dogs. See also Neapolitan mastiff; Tibetan mastiff. [Working Group]

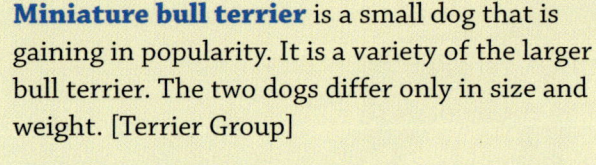

Miniature bull terrier is a small dog that is gaining in popularity. It is a variety of the larger bull terrier. The two dogs differ only in size and weight. [Terrier Group]

Miniature pinscher (PIN shuhr) is a small dog with a short, smooth coat. It looks like a small Doberman pinscher but is an older breed. Proud and peppy, it makes a playful pet and a good watchdog. *See also* Doberman pinscher; German pinscher. [Toy Group]

Miniature schnauzer (SHNOW zuhr) has a thick, wiry coat. A very popular dog, it is alert, active, and fond of children. *See also* Giant schnauzer; Standard schnauzer. [Terrier Group]

Neapolitan mastiff is a giant among dogs. "Neapolitan" refers to a farming area in southern Italy, where it was bred. This mastiff is especially known for its heavy, loose skin. Even though it walks slowly and seems lazy, it can quickly come to action if called upon to ward off intruders or otherwise protect its home. *See also* Mastiff; Tibetan mastiff. [Working Group]

Newfoundland is a huge dog with a long, full coat. Long known as a playmate and protector of children, this strong, fearless dog loves the water and has gained a reputation for rescuing people who are drowning. [Working Group]

Norfolk terrier was once considered the same breed as the Norwich terrier. Today they are separate breeds, differing only in how they carry their ears. The Norfolk's ears bend forward, while the Norwich's prick up. It makes an ideal pet. [Terrier Group]

Norwegian buhund (BOO *hund*), also known as the Norwegian sheepdog, originated in Norway, where it is still used mostly as a farm dog. Affectionate and active, it is good with children but needs a lot of exercise. [Miscellaneous Class]

Norwegian elkhound has a thick, gray coat. This dog was bred in Norway about 3,000 years ago to hunt elk. It has lots of energy, is very clean, and is a loyal family dog. [Hound Group]

Norwich terrier is named for Norwich, England. It was once considered the same breed as the Norfolk terrier. Today they are separate breeds, differing only in how they carry their ears. The Norwich's ears prick up, while the Norfolk's bend forward. [Terrier Group]

Nova Scotia duck tolling retriever is commonly called "the toller." As the name suggests, it originated in Nova Scotia, Canada. Not limited to retrieving ducks, it is well-rounded as a cheerful, loyal, loving, and protective pet. [Sporting Group]

Old English sheepdog has a heavy, shaggy coat that should be brushed regularly. This dog walks like a shuffling bear. An intelligent dog, the Old English sheepdog makes an excellent guard dog. [Herding Group]

Otterhound, bred in England to hunt otters, has a rough, thick coat. This hound is a fine swimmer and can work in cold water for long periods of time. [Hound Group]

Papillon (PAH *pee yohn*) has long, silky hair and a bushy tail. Its name is the French word for *butterfly,* and its ears do look a bit like a butterfly's wings. Dainty and lively, this dog is a loving pet. [Toy Group]

193

Parson Russell terrier is named after a minister named John Russell, who bred these dogs in England during the mid-1800's. Originally bred to hunt foxes, the breed now makes an energetic and affectionate pet. [Terrier Group]

Pekingese *(pee kihng EEZ)* was once the royal dog of China. It has been known outside China for only about 100 years. Stubborn and independent, but playful and loyal, the little Peke is a good family pet. [Toy Group]

Pembroke Welsh corgi *(KAWR gee)* has a dense, medium-length coat and a short tail. The name *corgi* is from two Welsh words meaning *dwarf dog*. The Pembroke is a good house dog. *See also* Cardigan Welsh corgi. [Herding Group]

Petit basset griffon vendéen *(peh TEE bah SAY grih FAHN vahn DAY uhn),* or PBGV or petit for short, dates to the 1500's in France. Its name, when translated from the French, means *small, low to the ground, and rough-coated*. Vendéen is an area in France where the breed developed. The petit is active, curious, and friendly. [Hound Group]

Pharaoh hound is one of the oldest breeds of dogs. Originally bred in Egypt, this dog was used in hunting. It has a short, glossy coat that is dark tan with some white markings. Affectionate and playful, this dog is good with children. [Hound Group]

Plott *(plaht)* is a breed of coonhound. A German immigrant to the United States named Johannes Plott developed it in the late 1700's to hunt bear, deer, and small game. The Plott is still an excellent hunter, as well as a loyal companion. [Hound Group]

Dogs to Know

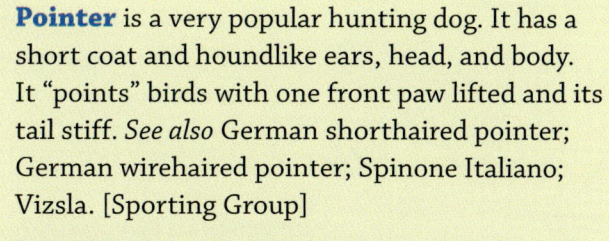

Pointer is a very popular hunting dog. It has a short coat and houndlike ears, head, and body. It "points" birds with one front paw lifted and its tail stiff. *See also* German shorthaired pointer; German wirehaired pointer; Spinone Italiano; Vizsla. [Sporting Group]

Polish lowland sheepdog probably originated in Central Asia, from the Tibetan terrier and other Asian dogs. The true breed developed in Poland under its Polish name, Polski Owczarek Nizinny, or PON for short. It nearly died out during World War II (1939-1945), but a Polish veterinarian saved the breed. The PON is a friendly family dog that loves children. [Herding Group]

Pomeranian is a small dog with a thick, fluffy coat. It is related to the strong sled dogs of Iceland and Lapland. Smart, lively, and even-tempered, the Pomeranian makes a good watchdog because of its sharp bark. [Toy Group]

Poodle is a very intelligent and popular dog. For shows, its thick, curly coat is clipped in one of the styles shown. There are three varieties of poodle—standard, miniature, and toy. [Non-sporting Group and Toy Group]

Portuguese water dog is named for its excellent swimming ability. It has webbed feet that allow it to swim long distances. It is used by fishing crews in Portugal to pull fish and nets from the ocean. [Working Group]

Pug, the largest dog in the Toy Group, has a soft, short coat, a black muzzle, and a tightly curled tail. The pug was probably bred in China and brought to Europe by the Dutch. For many years, it was a favorite in the Dutch and English royal courts. Alert and clean, pugs are mischievous, devoted, and easy to train. [Toy Group]

Puli *(poo lee)* is a medium-sized dog that has long been used by the shepherds of Hungary. Alert and active, the puli is a good guard dog. Its thick, shaggy coat tends to make the puli look larger than it is. [Herding Group]

Pyrenean shepherd *(pai REE nee uhn)* originated in the French Pyrenees Mountains. Originally a sheepherding dog, the Pyrenean shepherd became famous during World War I (1914-1918) when it carried messages across battlefields and helped find and rescue wounded soldiers. [Miscellaneous Class]

Redbone coonhound developed in Colonial America, when settlers needed hunting dogs to help them track animals to kill for food. The redbone has a keen sense of smell and loud bark. They are especially sure-footed, fast runners, but with their even temper, they can adjust well to home life. [Miscellaneous Class]

Retriever, *see* Chesapeake Bay retriever; Curly-coated retriever; Flat-coated retriever; Golden retriever; Labrador retriever.

Rhodesian ridgeback, or African lion hound, is a brave, swift hound with a short, sleek coat. A ridge of hair on its back that grows in the opposite direction to the rest of its coat gives this dog its name. Well-behaved, quiet, and easily trained, the Rhodesian is suited to country or city life. [Hound Group]

Rottweiler *(RAHT wy luhr),* named after the village in Germany where it was first bred, is descended from Roman cattle dogs. This dog's hair is short, coarse, and flat. The strong, brave, and calm rottweiler is a fine companion and guard dog. [Working Group]

Saint Bernard is famous for finding lost travelers in the snowy Swiss Alps. In addition to the familiar short-haired dog, there is also a long-haired variety. Saint Bernards are gentle, friendly dogs, but because of their large size, they must be carefully trained and supervised around children. [Working Group]

Saluki *(suh LOO kee)*, or gazelle hound, is thought to be the oldest purebred dog in the world. Named for the ancient Arabian city, the swift Saluki hunts by sight. The Saluki has a short, silky coat with feathering about the ears, legs, and tail. [Hound Group]

Samoyed *(sam uh YEHD)* comes from northern Siberia. The Samoyed people first bred this dog to guard reindeer herds and to pull sleds. Popular as a pet and watchdog, this big white dog with the "smiling" face is a loyal and intelligent animal. [Working Group]

Schnauzer, *see* Giant schnauzer; Miniature schnauzer; Standard schnauzer.

Schipperke *(SKIHP uhr kee)* has a heavy, black coat and may be born without a tail. It comes from Belgium, and its name means *little boatman.* It was once used to guard barges and to hurry the horses that pulled barges through Belgian canals. [Non-sporting Group]

Scottish deerhound is a very large, graceful hound with a harsh, wiry coat. First bred in Scotland as a royal hunting dog, it is now used to hunt game other than deer. A quiet dog and easy to train, the deerhound should have room to run. [Hound Group]

Scottish terrier, or "Scottie" as it is often called, is a small terrier. Its hard, wiry coat looks better when trimmed. Brave and alert, the Scottie is an excellent little hunter. Very popular as a pet, it is suited to life in a house or apartment. [Terrier Group]

Sealyham terrier is a small terrier with a wiry coat. It is named after the estate in Wales where it was first bred. The Sealyham has an even temper, is well-mannered, and is a good house dog. [Terrier Group]

Setter, see English setter; Gordon setter; Irish setter.

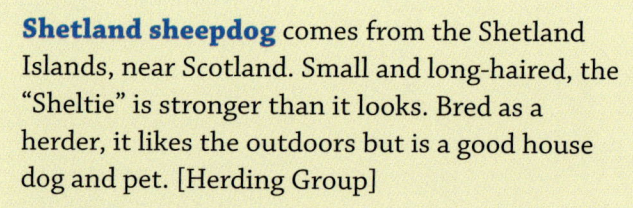

Shetland sheepdog comes from the Shetland Islands, near Scotland. Small and long-haired, the "Sheltie" is stronger than it looks. Bred as a herder, it likes the outdoors but is a good house dog and pet. [Herding Group]

Shiba inu (SHEE buh EE noo) is the smallest and oldest of the Japanese breeds. A dignified, good-natured dog, the shiba inu has an especially sharp sense of sight and smell. [Nonsporting Group]

Shih Tzu (shee dzoo) comes from Tibet and China. Its name, which is Chinese, means *lion dog*. Courageous and hardy, this little dog is always playful. Its long, dense coat may be any color. [Toy Group]

Siberian husky was bred in the Arctic as a sled dog. Naturally friendly, gentle, and clean, the Siberian is a good pet and companion. It is at home in the city or the country. [Working Group]

Silky terrier is an Australian dog. It has a long, silky coat and is related to the Australian and Yorkshire terriers. Friendly and curious, the silky terrier is an ideal house dog where space is limited. [Toy Group]

Skye terrier, one of the oldest of the many terrier breeds, comes from the Scottish island of Skye. This dog has a long, flowing coat that needs grooming. A bold hunter, the Skye is also a good watchdog. [Terrier Group]

Dogs to Know

Smooth fox terrier was once considered the same breed as the wire fox terrier. They were grouped together as fox terrier. Mischievous and playful, this dog is a popular pet. [Terrier Group]

Soft-coated wheaten terrier comes from Ireland. It has a shaggy coat of soft, wavy fur. The puppies have dark coats that turn the color of wheat in about two years. The wheaten likes children and is easily trained. [Terrier Group]

Spinone Italiano *(spee NOH nee ih tahl YAH noh)*, or Italian griffon, is a coarse-haired pointer. An all-purpose hunting dog, the Spinone also makes a devoted family dog. [Sporting Group]

Staffordshire bull terrier has a short, smooth coat. First bred in Staffordshire, England, as a fighting dog, it is fearless and obedient. *See also* American Staffordshire terrier. [Terrier Group]

Standard schnauzer *(SHNOW zuhr)* is the oldest of the three schnauzer breeds. Like the others, it has a thick, wiry coat, a beard, and bushy eyebrows. First known as a wirehaired pinscher, it takes its present name from a winning dog named Schnauzer. *See also* Giant schnauzer; Miniature schnauzer. [Working Group]

Sussex spaniel is named for the county of Sussex in England, where this dog was first bred. The Sussex is a strong, stocky dog, with short legs and a flat or slightly wavy coat. Unlike other spaniels, the Sussex often barks while it is hunting. It is a good, dependable gundog, makes a fine pet, and is excellent with children. [Sporting Group]

Swedish vallhund *(VAHL hoond)*, which means *herding dog,* has lived in Scandinavia for more than 1,000 years. It almost disappeared in the 1940's, but Swedish breeders have since revived the breed. It is best suited to farm or pasture life but is always eager to please an owner no matter where he or she may live. [Herding Group]

Tibetan mastiff is a big, furry dog from the Himalayan Mountains of Central Asia. A diplomat from the United Kingdom presented one of the dogs to Queen Victoria in 1847. Since then, the breed has gained popularity. This very protective dog is slow to make friends with people outside its own family. *See also* Mastiff; Neapolitan mastiff. [Working Group]

Tibetan spaniel, which is not a true spaniel, was kept by Buddhist monks. It has a thick, silky coat and a bushy tail. Its shoulders are covered with fur that is slightly longer than the rest of its coat. [Nonsporting Group]

Tibetan terrier is not a true terrier. Bred by Buddhist monks in the mountains of Tibet, it has a thick, shaggy coat and a fluffy tail that curls over its back. An active dog, the Tibetan enjoys both hot and cold weather. It makes an excellent family pet. [Nonsporting Group]

Toy fox terrier is a smooth fox terrier in miniature. Breeders in the United States crossed that breed with several toy breeds to get a dog that hunters could easily carry around in their saddlebags. They are good travelers and adapt well to almost any environment. [Toy Group]

Vizsla (*VEEZ lah*) is a medium-sized hunting dog with a short, smooth, rusty-gold coat. Also known as the Hungarian pointer and the yellow pointer, the Vizsla is named for a village in Hungary. The Vizsla hunts and tracks hare, points and retrieves game birds on land, and is also an excellent retriever in water. [Sporting Group]

Weimaraner (*VY muh rah nuhr*), a hunting dog from Weimar, Germany, has a sleek, gray coat. Nicknamed the "gray ghost," the Weimaraner moves smoothly in the field. This intelligent dog does very well in obedience trials and also loves to be part of the family. [Sporting Group]

Welsh corgi, *see* Cardigan Welsh corgi; Pembroke Welsh corgi.

Welsh springer spaniel is a very old breed of spaniel from Wales. It has a thick, silky, red-and-white coat that's straight or flat. The Welsh springer is a fine hunter and retriever that will work in the worst weather. Gentle with children, it is a good family dog. [Sporting Group]

Welsh terrier is a small, black-and-tan terrier from Wales. This dog has a wiry coat and looks like a small Airedale. A lively hunting dog, the quiet Welsh terrier also makes an excellent family pet and companion. [Terrier Group]

West Highland white terrier hails from the highlands of Scotland. It has a straight, tough coat that is easy to clean with a brush. A hardy outdoor dog, the Westie is also a good house pet. [Terrier Group]

Whippet is a small racing hound with a smooth coat that's easy to groom. Speedy and graceful, the whippet can run faster than any dog of the same weight. Quiet and dignified, it is a good family dog. [Hound Group]

Wire fox terrier for many years was considered the same breed as the smooth fox terrier. They were grouped together as the fox terrier. Friendly and playful, it is a popular pet. [Terrier Group]

Wirehaired pointing griffon is a hunting dog with a stiff, hard coat. A slow and careful hunter, the wirehaired griffon is also an excellent water dog that will work in all kinds of weather. [Sporting Group]

Yorkshire terrier is named for Yorkshire, England. You wouldn't think so to look at this dog, but the Yorkshire was bred to catch rats. Its long, silky hair needs special grooming for show purposes. [Toy Group]

Find Out More

Ages 5 to 8

American Kennel Club for Kids

http://www.akc.org/kids_juniors/index.cfm?nav_area=kids_juniors

An AKC Web site that offers a newsletter, contest, and fun activities.

Arthur's New Puppy by Marc Brown (Little, Brown, 1993)

Arthur the aardvark gets a mischievous puppy and has to learn how to train it. Also by the same author: *Arthur's Pet Business.*

Checkerboard Animal Library: Dogs by Julie Murray and Nancy Furstinger (ABDO Publishing, 2003-2006)

Each book in this series of 12 titles describes a certain breed, according to its personality, physical traits, and care and feeding requirements.

Harry the Dirty Dog by Gene Zion (Harper and Row, 1956)

Why is Harry begging for a hated bath? Other classics in the series: *Harry and the Lady Next Door, Harry by the Sea,* and *No Roses for Harry.*

Kizzy by Chris Williams (Moo Press, 2006)

A day in the life of Kizzy, a special kind of therapy dog. Kizzy visits children and adults with reading and speaking difficulties and helps them feel comfortable reading to him.

Woof! It's a Dog's Life

http://www.pbs.org/wgbh/woof/index.html

Matthew Margolis from the Public Broadcasting System answers questions and gives advice on choosing and training a dog and dealing with behavior problems.

Ages 9 to 12

American Kennel Club for Juniors

http://www.akc.org/kids_juniors/index.cfm?nav_area=kids_juniors

An AKC Web site that offers a newsletter, contest, and fun activities.

The Complete Dog Book by the American Kennel Club, 20th edition (Ballantine Books, 2006)

Describes every breed admitted to the American Kennel Club registration at the time of publication. It also includes information on each breed's history and official standards for dog shows, plus tips on the care, breeding, and training of purebred dogs.

Dogs: A Natural History by Jake Page (HarperCollins, 2007)

Did we domesticate dogs—or did it happen the other way around? Find the answer here, along with many other revelations about dogs and their wild ancestors, the wolves.

The Incredible Journey by Sheila Burnford (Little, Brown, 1961)

The classic story of a Siamese cat, an English bull terrier, and a Labrador retriever who find their way home through the Canadian wilderness.

Janet Wall's How to Love Your Dog: A Kid's Guide to Dog Care

http://loveyourdog.com

Includes the essentials of caring for a dog, safety tips, stories about dogs, and suggestions for careers with dogs.

Kennel Club Dog Breed series (Kennel Club Books, 2003-)

Each book in this set of over 100 titles describes a particular breed and how to raise it.

My Life in Dog Years by Gary Paulsen (Delacorte Press, 1998)

Paulsen retells his life in terms of the dogs he's owned, among them Snowball, his first dog while living in the Philippines; Ike, his hunting companion; Dirk, who protected him from bullies; and Cookie, who saved his life.

Old Yeller by Fred Gipson (Harper, 1956)

This classic story of the Texas frontier tells how 13-year-old Travis comes to love and depend on Old Yeller, a big, ugly mutt, until their life together ends in tragedy.

Find Out More

Glossary

apron The frill of hair below the neck and on the chest of a long-haired dog such as the collie.

bay The long, deep sound a hound makes when it is hunting.

beard The very bushy whiskers on the muzzle and lower jaw of some breeds, such as the bearded collie.

bench show A show at which dogs competing for prizes are "benched"—that is, kept on a bench before and after judging.

best in show The top award at a dog show, the one given to the dog judged the best of all the dogs in the show.

best of breed The award given at a dog show to each dog that is judged to be the best of a particular breed.

bitch An adult female dog.

blaze A white stripe down the middle of the face, between the eyes.

brindle *(BRIHN duhl)* A color of coat, caused by a mixture of light and dark hairs.

canine *(KAY nyn)* A word that means dog or doglike. Also, any one of the group of meat-eating animals that includes dogs, foxes, wolves, coyotes, and jackals.

canines *(KAY nyns)* The two long, pointed teeth, or fangs, in the upper and lower jaws. The upper canine teeth are called the eyeteeth.

choke collar A chain or leather collar that tightens when pulled.

crossbred A dog who is a mixture of two or more kinds of dogs.

dam The female parent; the mother dog.

dewclaw An extra claw above the paw, like a fifth toe, on the inside of the forelegs and sometimes on the inside of the hind legs.

dock To shorten a dog's tail by cutting part of it off. A docked tail is a standard for some breeds, such as the Doberman pinscher.

dog An adult male dog. The term is also used for all dogs, both male and female.

dragsman A person who runs ahead in a certain type of fox hunt, dragging a fox-scented sack for the dogs to follow.

elbow The joint in the front leg between the upper arm and the forearm.

eyeteeth The two long, pointed teeth in the upper jaw. *See also* canines.

fall The long hair hanging down over the face of a dog such as the Skye terrier.

feathering The long fringe of hair on the ears, legs, or tail of some breeds, such as the English setter.

field trial A contest for breeds in the Sporting Group and for some hounds. The dogs are judged by their ability and style in finding or retrieving animals, or following a scent.

flush To drive, or spring, a bird or other animal from cover, forcing it to fly or run.

groom To brush, comb, or trim a dog's coat.

handler A person who shows a dog at a dog show or works a dog at a field trial.

hard mouth A dog that leaves teeth marks in the birds and animals it retrieves is said to have a hard mouth. This is a serious fault in a retriever. *See also* soft mouth.

harlequin *(HAHR luh kin)* A coat, such as that of a harlequin Great Dane, with odd-shaped patches of color, usually black on white.

heat The time when a female is able to have puppies. This happens twice a year.

heel A command at which a dog must stay in position at its handler's side.

height The height of a dog, called shoulder height, is measured from the ground to the withers. *See also* withers.

hock The joint in a dog's hind leg. The hock is a dog's true heel.

hound Any one of the dogs that hunt by sight or by scent.

incisors *(ihn SY zuhrs)* The six upper and six lower front teeth, between the canines.

kennel A house or enclosed space where dogs are kept; also a place where dogs are bred or boarded.

length The length of a dog's body is measured from the forechest to the back of the thigh.

litter All the puppies born at one time to a mother dog.

mascot An animal, person, or thing that is supposed to bring good luck.

mask Dark coloring, like a mask, on the front part of the head.

mate To bring a male and female together so that a litter of puppies may be born. *See also* dog; bitch; litter.

milk teeth A puppy's first teeth.

mixed breed A dog whose mother or father was of two or more breeds.

mongrel A dog whose mother and father were both mixed breeds.

muzzle The part of the head in front of the eyes. Also, a leather strap or wire cage put on a dog's muzzle to keep the dog from biting or eating.

obedience trial *(oh BEE dee uhns)* An event in which dogs compete to show how well they have learned to obey. Obedience degrees are earned at these trials.

pads The cushions, or soles, of a dog's paws.

pedigree *(PEHD uh gree)* The written record of a dog's ancestors. The American Kennel Club can supply pedigrees for all registered dogs.

point A stance that certain breeds of hunting dogs take to indicate to the hunter that the dog has located a bird.

pointer A type of hunting dog bred and trained to find birds and signal its discovery to the hunter, often by raising its foreleg and "pointing" at the bird with its muzzle.

puppy Any dog less than 1 year old.

purebred A dog with ancestors of the same breed.

register To send information about your dog to an official organization such as the American Kennel Club. The organization will record the information and assign a special number to the dog.

retriever A type of hunting dog bred and trained to retrieve (bring back) a bird or animal that has been shot.

ruff The band of thick, long hair that grows around the neck of a dog such as a chow chow.

setter A type of dog used to find birds. A setter usually points with its nose, but it may also lift one front leg. Setters were developed from a hunting dog called a setting spaniel that was trained to "set"(crouch or lie down) when it found birds, so that a net could be thrown over the birds to capture them. There are three breeds of setters: English, Gordon, and Irish.

sire *(syr)* The male parent; the father dog.

soft mouth A dog that retrieves birds and animals without damaging them with teeth marks is said to have a soft mouth. *See also* hard mouth.

spaniel *(SPAN yuhl)* A type of dog. The spaniel family contains more breeds than any other. The name *spaniel* comes from the word *Spain,* the country where these dogs were probably first developed.

spay To operate on a female dog so she can't have puppies.

studbook A book containing the pedigrees and records of registered dogs. *See also* pedigree; register.

terrier Any one of a group of dogs once bred to drive small animals out of burrows, or holes, in the ground. The name *terrier* comes from the Latin word *terra,* meaning *earth.*

umbilical cord The tubelike structure that connects an unborn puppy to its mother, providing nourishment until the puppy is born. The mother dog chews off the umbilical cord at birth, leaving the puppy with a small scar—a bellybutton.

veterinarian An animal doctor.

wean *(ween)* To get a puppy used to food other than its mother's milk.

whelp A puppy that still takes milk from its mother. Also, to give birth to a litter of puppies.

withers The highest point of the shoulders, just behind the neck. A dog's height (called *shoulder height)* is measured to the withers.

Index

This index is an alphabetical list of important topics covered in this book. It will help you find information given in both words and pictures. To help you understand what an entry means, there is sometimes a helping word in parentheses, for example, **dam** (female dog). If there is information in both words and pictures, you will see the words *with pictures* in parentheses after the page number. If there is only a picture, you will see the word *picture* in parentheses after the page number.

A

affenpinscher, 176 *(with picture)*
AKC. *See* **American Kennel Club**
Akita, 177 *(with picture)*
all-breed show, 130
American Coon Hunters Association, 30
American Kennel Club, 22, 23, 30, 52-53, 130, 131, 134, 176
art, 104-109 *(with pictures)*
assistance dog, 114-119 *(with pictures)*
Australian Aborigines, 142-143 *(with picture)*

B

Balto (dog), 94-101 *(with pictures)*
Barry (dog), 35, 90-91 *(with pictures)*
basenji, 30 *(with picture),* 178 *(with picture)*
bathing of dogs, 164
beagle, 135, 157 *(picture),* 163 *(picture),* 178 *(with picture)*
beauceron, 52, 179 *(with picture)*
bedding, 163 *(with picture)*
Beethoven (dog), 128 *(with picture)*
bellybutton, on dog, 167
benched show, 130
Benji (dog), 128
bichon frise, 47 *(with picture),* 180 *(with picture)*
bird hunting, 25-27 *(with pictures),* 135-136 *(with pictures)*
bitch, 131
bloodhound, 121-123 *(with picture),* 180 *(with picture)*
borzoi, 79, 181 *(with picture)*
Bosch, Michael, 92-93 *(with picture)*
bouvier des Flandres, 181 *(with picture)*
boxer, 121, 181 *(with picture)*
breed and breeding, 20-23 *(with pictures),* 176-201 *(with pictures)*
  new, 78-81 *(with pictures)*
  old, 72-77 *(with pictures)*
  origin of, 69-71
briard, 38-39, 181 *(with picture)*
Brittany, 182 *(with picture)*
Buddy (dog), 128-129 *(with picture)*
buhund, Norwegian, 53 *(picture),* 193 *(with picture)*
bull-baiting, 44-45
bulldog, 44-45 *(with picture),* 100, 182 *(with picture)*
  English, 22, 81
  French, 186 *(with picture)*
bullmastiff, 182 *(with picture)*
bull terrier, 50 *(with picture),* 88-89 *(with picture),* 182 *(with picture)*
  miniature, 192 *(with picture)*
  Staffordshire, 199 *(with picture)*

C

Canaan dog, 182 *(with picture)*
cattle dog, 125
  Australian, 125, 178 *(with picture)*

Celts, 76 *(with picture)*
Cephalus (hunter), 148-149 *(with picture)*
Cerberus (dog), 144-145 *(with picture)*
chihuahua, 41, 69, 159 *(picture),* 183 *(with picture)*
chin, Japanese, 42, 190 *(with picture)*
China, 41-42, 46, 74, 107 *(picture)*
chow chow, 21, 45 *(picture),* 46, 74, 183 *(with picture)*
coat, 160 *(with pictures)*
cocker spaniel, 92-93 *(with pictures),* 164 *(picture),* 184 *(with picture)*
  English, 185 *(with picture)*
collie, 20-21, 36 *(with picture),* 127-128 *(with picture),* 136, 184 *(with picture)*
  bearded, 179 *(with picture)*
  border, 125 *(with picture),* 157 *(picture),* 181 *(with picture)*
conformation show. *See* **dog show**
Conroy, John Robert, 88-89
coonhound, 30 *(with picture)*
  black and tan, 30 *(with picture),* 180 *(with picture)*
  redbone, 196 *(with picture)*
corgi, 36, 136
  See also **Welsh corgi**
coursing, 137
crested dog, Chinese, 183 *(with picture)*
crossbred, 20-22 *(with pictures)*
Crufts (dog show), 132

205

D

dachshund, 70, 71, 79-80 *(with pictures),* 135, 184 *(with picture)*
Dalmatian, 46-47 *(with picture),* 157, 184 *(with picture)*
dam (female dog), 156
deerhound, Scottish, 197 *(with picture)*
degree for dog, 133-134
Diana (goddess), 148 *(with picture)*
docking, 161
doghouse, 163
Dogrib Indians, 150-151 *(with picture)*
dogs, origin of, 67-69
dog show, 130-132 *(with pictures)*
Dogue de Bordeaux, 53 *(picture),* 185 *(with picture)*

E

Egypt, ancient, 74-75 *(with picture),* 104 *(with picture)*
elkhound, Norwegian, 30, 70, 73 *(with picture),* 193 *(with picture)*
Eskimo dog, American, 177 *(with picture)*

F

feeding of dogs, 162 *(with picture)*
field trial, 135-136 *(with pictures)*
Four-Legs (dog), 56-65 *(with pictures)*
foxhound
 American, 28, 177 *(with picture)*
 English, 28 *(with picture),* 185 *(with picture)*
fox hunting, 28 *(with picture)*
fox terrier
 smooth, 199 *(with picture)*
 toy, 200 *(with picture)*
 wire, 201 *(with picture)*
Frederick the Great, 43

G

German shepherd, 21, 70, 100, 186 *(with picture)*
 work by, 38, 39 *(with picture),* 114, 121 *(with picture),* 123 *(with picture),* 125, 128 *(with picture),* 136
Germany, 78-80
goldendoodle, 20 *(with picture)*
Googoorewon (place), 142-143 *(with picture)*
Great Dane, 78-79, 159 *(picture),* 188 *(with picture)*
Great Pyrenees, 188 *(with picture)*
Greeks, ancient, 77 *(with picture),* 104, 106 *(picture),* 144 *(with picture)*
Greyfriars' Bobby (dog), 56-65 *(with pictures)*
greyhound, 31, 75 *(with pictures),* 137, 188 *(with picture)*
 Italian, 43 *(with picture),* 77, 190 *(with picture)*
griffon, 194 *(with picture)*
 Brussels, 182 *(with picture)*
 wirehaired pointing, 201 *(with picture)*
grooming of dogs, 164 *(with picture)*
guide dog, 114-117 *(with pictures)*

H

Hades (god), 144
harrier, 188 *(with picture)*
Havanese, 188 *(with picture)*
hearing by dogs, 158-159
hearing ear dog. *See* **signal dog**
Henry III of France, 47
Hercules (hero), 144-145 *(with picture)*
Herding Group, 22, 36-39 *(with pictures),* 131, 136-137
Honey (dog), 92-93 *(with pictures)*

hound, 28-31 *(with pictures)*
 Afghan, 161 *(picture),* 176 *(with picture)*
 basset, 135, 178 *(with picture)*
 Ibizan, 75, 189 *(with picture)*
 pharaoh, 75, 194 *(with picture)*
 Rhodesian ridgeback, 137
 See also **bloodhound; coonhound; dachshund; deerhound, Scottish; elkhound, Norwegian; foxhound; greyhound; otterhound; wolfhound**
Hound Group, 22, 28-31 *(with pictures),* 131
housebreaking of dogs, 165 *(with picture)*
hunting, 25-28 *(with pictures),* 72-76 *(with pictures),* 135-137 *(with pictures)*
husky, Siberian, 33-34, 70, 138, 198 *(with picture)*

I

Iditarod (race), 138-139 *(with picture)*

J

Japan, 146-147 *(with picture)*

K

Kaasen, Gunnar, 95-101 *(with picture)*
Keeshond, 190 *(with picture)*
komondor, 125, 190 *(with picture)*
kuvasz, 190 *(with picture)*

L

language, dogs in, 110, 111
Lassie (dog), 36, 127-128 *(with picture)*
leash, 166-167, 173
Lelaps (dog), 148-149 *(with picture)*
lhasa apso, 191 *(with picture)*
litter, 22, 156 *(with picture)*

lost dogs, 173
löwchen, 191 *(with picture)*

M

malamute, Alaskan, 33-34, 70, 138, 177 *(with picture)*
Malinois, Belgian, 179 *(with picture)*
Maltese, 77 *(with pictures),* 191 *(with picture)*
Marc, Franz, 109 *(picture)*
mastiff, 75, 191 *(with picture)*
  Neapolitan, 192 *(with picture)*
  Tibetan, 52, 200 *(with picture)*
  See also **bullmastiff**
mating, 20, 70-71, 156
microchip, 173
Miscellaneous Class, 22, 52-53 *(with pictures)*
mongrel, 21-22
mountain dog
  Bernese, 33 *(with picture),* 180 *(with picture)*
  Greater Swiss, 188 *(with picture)*
mutation, 69
mutt. See **mongrel**

N

Nepomuk, St. John, 108 *(picture)*
Newfoundland dog, 35 *(with picture),* 80, 123, 192 *(with picture)*
Nonsporting Group, 22, 44-47 *(with pictures),* 131

O

obedience trial, 133-134 *(with picture)*
otterhound, 78 *(with pictures),* 193 *(with picture)*

P

Pal (dog), 127
papillon, 42 *(with picture),* 193 *(with picture)*
Pekingese, 41-42, 71, 194 *(with picture)*
performing dog, 126-129 *(with pictures)*

petit basset griffon vendéen, 194 *(with picture)*
pinscher, 174 *(with picture)*
  Doberman, 43, 80, 121, 185 *(with picture)*
  German, 186 *(with picture)*
  miniature, 43, 192 *(with picture)*
Plott, 52, 194 *(with picture)*
pointer, 25 *(with picture),* 135, 195 *(with picture)*
  English, 135 *(picture)*
  German shorthaired, 187 *(with picture)*
  German wirehaired, 187 *(with picture)*
police dog, 120-121 *(with pictures)*
Pomeranian, 195 *(with picture)*
poodle, 20 *(with picture),* 45-46 *(with picture),* 195 *(with picture)*
  miniature, 44 *(picture),* 46
  standard, 46
  toy, 43, 46
proverb, 110
pug, 41 *(with picture),* 69, 160 *(picture),* 195 *(with picture)*
puli, 36, 38 *(picture),* 125, 196 *(with picture)*
puppy
  birth of, 156-157 *(with pictures)*
  choosing, 154-155
  feeding, 162
  housebreaking, 165 *(picture)*
purebred, 20-22 *(with pictures),* 154

R

retriever, 27 *(with picture),* 135-136 *(with picture)*
  Chesapeake Bay, 27 *(picture),* 80-81 *(with pictures),* 183 *(with picture)*
  curly-coated, 184 *(with picture)*
  flat-coated, 186 *(with picture)*
  golden, 20 *(with picture),* 114, 121, 123, 128-129 *(with picture),* 156 *(picture),* 187 *(with picture)*

Labrador, 23, 100, 114, 121, 123, 136 *(picture),* 191 *(with picture)*
Nova Scotia duck tolling, 193 *(with picture)*
ridgeback, Rhodesian, 137, 196 *(with picture)*
Rin-Tin-Tin (dog), 128 *(with picture)*
Rome, ancient, 105, 107 *(picture),* 148
rottweiler, 81, 125, 136, 196 *(with picture)*
rudder (tail), 161
Russia, 79, 81

S

Saint Bernard, 22 *(picture),* 34-35, 90-91 *(with pictures),* 128 *(with picture),* 197 *(with picture)*
Saluki, 31, 75, 137, 197 *(with picture)*
Samoyed, 34 *(with picture),* 136, 138, 197 *(with picture)*
schipperke, 197 *(with picture)*
schnauzer
  giant, 81, 187 *(with picture)*
  miniature, 192 *(with picture)*
  standard, 199 *(with picture)*
Scott, Sir Walter, 48-50
search-and-rescue dog, 122-123 *(with pictures)*
seeing eye dog. See **guide dog**
seizure alert dog, 118
service dog, 114, 117-119 *(with picture)*
setter, 25 *(with picture),* 135
  English, 24 *(picture),* 135 *(picture),* 185 *(with picture)*
  Gordon, 187 *(with picture)*
  Irish, 20-21, 133 *(picture),* 189 *(with picture)*
  Irish red and white, 52 *(picture),* 189 *(with picture)*
shar-pei, Chinese, 183 *(with picture)*
sheepdog, 36-39 *(with pictures),* 124-125 *(with picture),* 136-137

207

Belgian, 125, 179 *(with picture)*
Old English, 125, 193 *(with picture)*
Polish lowland, 195 *(with picture)*
Shetland, 198 *(with picture)*
shepherd dog
Anatolian, 178 *(with picture)*
Australian, 178 *(with picture)*
Pyrenean, 53 *(picture)*, 196 *(with picture)*
white Siberian, 109 *(picture)*
See also **German shepherd**
shiba inu, 198 *(with picture)*
Shih Tzu, 42 *(with picture)*, 155 *(picture)*, 198 *(with picture)*
Shiro (dog), 146-147 *(with picture)*
shots, 154, 171
sighthound, 137
sight hunting, 137
signal dog, 114, 117
sire, 156
sled-dog racing, 138-139 *(with picture)*
smell, sense of, 24, 30, 100, 122-123, 158
spaniel, 26 *(with picture)*, 42, 135
Cavalier King Charles, 109 *(picture)*, 183 *(with picture)*
Clumber, 183 *(with picture)*
English toy, 185 *(with picture)*
field, 186 *(with picture)*
Sussex, 199 *(with picture)*
Tibetan, 200 *(with picture)*
See also **cocker spaniel; springer spaniel; water spaniel**
special needs dog, 114, 118-119 *(with picture)*
Spinone Italiano, 199 *(with picture)*
spitz, Finnish, 186 *(with picture)*
Sporting Group, 22, 25-27 *(with pictures)*, 131
springer spaniel
English, 26 *(with picture)*, 132 *(picture)*, 185 *(with picture)*
Welsh, 201 *(with picture)*
Stubby (dog), 88-89 *(with pictures)*
studbook, 30

T

tags, for dog, 171, 173 *(with picture)*
tail, 160-161
teeth, 159
terrier, 48-51 *(with pictures)*
Airedale, 50-51 *(with picture)*, 81, 121, 176 *(with picture)*
American Staffordshire, 177 *(with picture)*
Australian, 51 *(with picture)*, 178 *(with picture)*
Bedlington, 179 *(with picture)*
Black Russian, 81, 180 *(with picture)*
border, 181 *(with picture)*
Boston, 22, 81, 181 *(with picture)*
cairn, 48 *(with picture)*, 182 *(with picture)*
Dandie Dinmont, 48 *(picture)*, 50, 184 *(with picture)*
English, 22, 81
Glen of Imaal, 187 *(with picture)*
Irish, 189 *(with picture)*
Kerry blue, 190 *(with picture)*
lakeland, 191 *(with picture)*
Manchester, 51 *(picture)*, 191 *(with picture)*
Norfolk, 192 *(with picture)*
Norwich, 193 *(with picture)*
Parson Russell, 194 *(with picture)*
Scottish, 160 *(picture)*, 197 *(with picture)*
Sealyham, 198 *(with picture)*
silky, 198 *(with picture)*
Skye, 84-87 *(with pictures)*, 198 *(with picture)*
soft-coated wheaten, 199 *(with picture)*
Tibetan, 200 *(with picture)*
toy-sized Manchester, 43
Welsh, 201 *(with picture)*
West Highland white, 201 *(with picture)*
Yorkshire, 201 *(with picture)*
See also **bull terrier; fox terrier**
Terrier Group, 22, 48-51 *(with pictures)*, 131
Tervuren, Belgian, 179 *(with picture)*

therapy dog, 119 *(with picture)*
tongue, 160
Toy Group, 22, 41-43 *(with pictures)*, 131
training of dogs, 166-170 *(with pictures)*
traveling with dogs, 172 *(with picture)*

U

umbilical cord, 156, 167
Ur (ancient city), 104

V

vallhund, Swedish, 52, 199 *(with picture)*
veterinarian, 154, 171 *(with picture)*
Vizsla, 200 *(with picture)*

W

water dog, Portuguese, 195 *(with picture)*
water spaniel
American, 177 *(with picture)*
Irish, 189 *(with picture)*
weaning, 157
Weatherwax, Rudd, 127
Weimaraner, 200 *(with picture)*
Welsh corgi
Cardigan, 39 *(picture)*, 76 *(with pictures)*, 125, 182 *(with picture)*
Pembroke, 125, 194 *(with picture)*
Westminster Kennel Club Show, 131-132 *(with picture)*
whippet, 137, 161 *(picture)*, 201 *(with picture)*
wolf, 124, 159-160
gray, 67-72 *(with picture)*
wolfhound
Irish, 31 *(with picture)*, 76, 137, 189 *(with picture)*
Russian, see **borzoi**
Working Group, 22, 33-35 *(with pictures)*, 131, 135-137 *(with pictures)*